MAN CITY
CITY
50 CLASSIC
MATCHES

and some to forget!

DAVID CLAYTON

The History Press

Dedication

Dedicated to the memory of little Frankie Dean.

Acknowledgements

Thanks to my commissioning editor Michelle Tilling at The History Press. Thanks too, to my family, the *Manchester Evening News* for allowing me to use photographs, *City Magazine* and the club for supporting whatever I've been involved with over the years.

I wrote this book in between moving homes and but for the patience shown by my wife Sarah and my three beautiful children, Harry, Jaimé and Chrissie, it wouldn't have been possible.

First published 2010

The History Press
The Mill, Brimscombe Port
Stroud, Gloucestershire, GL5 2QG
www.thehistorypress.co.uk

British Library Cataloguing in Publication Data.
A catalogue record for this book is available from the British
Library.

ISBN 978 0 7524 5559 4

Typesetting and origination by The History Press
Printed in Great Britain

Contents

Introduction

L et's face it, every City game is not a classic match, but it's fair to say that of all the matches the Blues have ever played, each one is special to somebody for different reasons. Maybe it was the first game they saw, or perhaps something happened the same day City were playing that makes a game that means not that much to the majority of supporters mean a lot to somebody else.

Personally, I can associate dozens, maybe hundreds of memories around particular games, some memorable, others very forgetful. There's stuff that's stuck in my mind that has no logical explanation, too. I can remember watching a lamp blowing in the Kippax roof on a windy evening when we played Northampton Town in the League Cup in the early 1980s. I remember sitting terrified as a kid in the Main Stand next to 300 of West Ham's ICF firm that had somehow got tickets in there and feeling relieved when Paul Goddard scored a late winner for them.

There was a time when I saw a Sheffield Wednesday fan who had been stabbed outside the main entrance prior to a cup match in 1979, a victim perhaps of one of the Blues' notorious hooligan firms, and ten years later getting caught in a car with my brother as bricks were thrown around us as City and Millwall fans waged war on Yew Tree Road. There was a time I went with my primary school and sat on the front row of the North Stand as John Richards scored twice to give Wolves a 2–0 win in 1977 – my second game as a City fan – and I left wondering whether I'd be able to take another defeat.

I've been chased at Blackburn and Everton while minding my own business and been present when Paul Lake swallowed his tongue and everyone thought he was going to die right in front of us on the Maine Road pitch.

My memorable games won't necessarily be yours, but we'll share a lot of the same ones, I'm certain. Beating the Rags 5–1, putting ten past Huddersfield, the 1981 FA Cup semi-final against Ipswich, the Gillingham play-off final, Blackburn away to clinch promotion in 2000, beating Sheffield Wednesday 6–2 at Hillsborough in 2001, Kinky's debut, Goat robbing Neville to score, taking my son to his first game . . . it goes on and on and I'm privileged to say I was there on each occasion, including Luton in 1983, AC Milan in 1978 and the night David White scored four at Villa Park.

The point is, I've chosen fifty games here that I hope will evoke great memories for you all – they certainly did for me, but if there's a couple of seemingly random matches in here that leave you scratching your head, it's because this book is about Manchester City and therefore elements of unpredictability are not merely indulgent, more mandatory.

At the end of the book there are several Top 20 lists and 10 Matches to Forget. Because I'd like this to be a book you dip in and out of, you might find a little repetition within these lists, but forgive me for this – occasionally a match or incident is worth mentioning more than once!

David Clayton, Manchester, 2010

1 The Italian Job

AC MILAN 2, CITY 2
DATE: 23 NOVEMBER 1978
COMPETITION: UEFA CUP ROUND 3
CITY: CORRIGAN, CLEMENTS, DONACHIE, BOOTH, WATSON, POWER,
VILJOEN, BELL, KIDD, HARTFORD, PALMER SUBS: MACRAE, KEEGAN,
HENRY, COUGHLIN, P. FUTCHER

*Where was the author? Listening to a radio smuggled into the fourth form
biology class at Parrs Wood High and owned by our school goalie, Chris
Simpson.*

When a thick fog descended on the magnificent San Siro Stadium in Milan just a few hours before kick-off, the officials had no choice but to call the match off. The game was rescheduled for the following afternoon – something that today's multi-million television moguls would never sanction – and on 23 November 1978, Manchester City ran out to the glorious sight of one of the world's best venues bathed in warm autumn sunshine.

Just a handful of the 1,000 or so Blues who had made the journey to Italy stayed on for the game which still attracted 60,000, but the atmosphere was less hostile – the crowd was muted and there were no firecrackers to be heard or flares to be seen.

Milan had never lost to a British side on their own turf and were the strong favourites to continue that record. City, managed by Tony Book, were having a decidedly average season and though victories in the previous rounds against FC Twente and Standard Liege proved the team were capable of better things on their day, Milan were an entirely different proposition.

Predictably, the hosts started by putting City immediately under pressure, and while the Italians never missed an opportunity to ruffle City's feathers, they found the towering partnership of Tommy Booth and Dave Watson in fine form. Milan soon became frustrated after failing to find an early breakthrough. Asa Hartford was starting to run things in the middle and when he floated a perfect cross over to the far post, Brian Kidd gave the Blues an unlikely lead. Unbelievably, the lunchtime kick-off meant that as the half-time whistle blew, the majority of City fans had to leave the stadium to catch their plane home!

With virtually no City vocal support left inside the San Siro, Milan came back strongly and had the ball in the net almost straight from the restart, but it was ruled out for offside. City weathered frantic pressure as the

Brian Kidd makes it 3–0 in the return match against AC Milan in 1978.

Italians fought to stay in the tie, but in the 57th minute, the Blues again silenced the home crowd by doubling their lead. Paul Power picked the ball up just outside his own area and then began a surge forward. Pretty much unchallenged, he continued to the edge of the Milan box and fired in a weak shot that bobbled twice before deceiving Albertosi and nestling in the net to make it 2–0. City needed to get the ball and kill the game for the next 15 minutes if they were to pull off a famous win, but instead they let Milan pull one back almost straight from the kick-off through Bigon. He had the ball in the net again four minutes later as Book's side suddenly looked vulnerable and edgy, but the linesman's flag came to the rescue and it was ruled offside. The Italians were building up an impressive head of steam and their volatile fans, stirred by the comeback, began throwing missiles at Joe Corrigan in the City goal.

It seemed inevitable that Milan would draw level and on 83 minutes, they finally did thanks again to Bigon. Thoughts of victory banished, the Blues were forced to hang on for dear life as Milan pressed for a winner, but there were no more goals and the game ended 2–2 – still a fantastic result and one of the Blues' best in European football – and there was even better to come. City won the second leg 3–0 with an exhilarating display that should have given the team confidence to go on and win the cup, but an unfortunate draw saw City paired with Germany's Borussia Mönchengladbach and an eventual 2–4 aggregate defeat. It was to be Tony Book's last season in charge and City finished in 15th position in the league, crashing out of the FA Cup to Shrewsbury Town. Nobody, however, would forget memory of Milan.

2   Poles Apart

City 2, Gornik Zabrze 1
Date: 29 April 1970
Competition: European Cup Winners' Cup Final
City: Corrigan, Book, Pardoe, Doyle (Bowyer), Booth, Oakes,
Heslop, Lee, Young, Bell, Towers
Att: 7,968

Where was the author? Probably asleep in bed with my teddy!

The Blues' triumph in Vienna remains the only European trophy the club have so far collected, but then again, only a handful can actually lay claim to a major European trophy. In today's weird world of European football, where groups play out phases, losers go into another competition and the dear old Cup Winners' Cup no longer exists, City's success was won the old-fashioned way, randomly drawn out of a hat and over two-legged knock-out rounds.

City qualified by winning the 1969 FA Cup and were playing in Europe for the second successive year after taking part in the European Cup the previous season, falling at the first hurdle. That time, Malcolm Allison had boasted how his side would 'terrify Europe' only to see Turkish side Fenerbahçe edge the tie 2–1 on aggregate in what was a major shock. The disappointment and embarrassment felt by the players was obvious and they were determined to prove that they were among the very best on the continent next time around.

The tournament began in earnest with a qualifying round between Rapid Vienna and Torpedo Moscow. Both games finished in draws with Vienna progressing to the next phase on the away goals rule. The first round proper was then drawn and City couldn't have asked for a much tougher test, pitted against Atletico Bilbao. Gornik Zabrze of Poland drew Olympiakos of Greece while Rapid Vienna, with the added incentive of the final being in their home city, took on PSV Eindhoven.

City seemed to be on their way out when Bilbao opened up a 2–0 lead in the first leg in Spain. The Blues pulled a goal back, but again went two goals behind but despite pulling a goal back, slipped to 3–1 with time rapidly running out. But they didn't give up, and two late goals from Tommy Booth and an own goal gave them a fantastic 3–3 draw. It was just the fillip they needed after Fenerbahçe.

Gornik drew 2–2 in Greece while Rapid's hopes nose-dived with a 2–1 home loss to PSV. Elsewhere, Belgians SK Lierse trounced Cypriots

APOEL Nicosia 10–1, while Cardiff City thrashed Mjøndalen IF 7–1 in Norway and Rangers beat Steaua Bucharest 2–0 at Ibrox.

For the return at Maine Road, goals from Colin Bell, Alan Oakes and Ian Bowyer eased City into the second round 3–0 and 6–3 on aggregate. Gornik won 5–0 against Olympiakos; Cardiff completed the rout of the Norwegian minnows 5–1 at Ninian Park; Rangers held out for a 0–0 draw in Romania and Rapid dipped out 4–2 at PSV. The next round would prove equally fascinating.

The Blues were then drawn against the first round's top-scorers, with the first leg away against Belgians SK Lierse, who had banged in eleven goals and were something of an unknown quantity.

A 19,000 crowd packed into the Herman Vanderpoortenstadion with the local hopes high of an upset. Franny Lee and Bell had other ideas, however, and City coasted home 3–0. Gornik saw off Glasgow Rangers 3–1 in Poland, while Göztepe of Turkey all but ended Cardiff's hopes with a 3–0 win.

The second legs would see the end of all British interest bar City, who finished off the job against Lierse by scoring five without reply in front of 26,486 fans at Maine Road. Cardiff made a valiant bid to overturn their deficit but 1–0 was not enough, while Rangers went down to the inspired Gornik 3–1.

Elsewhere, German side Schalke 04 and Portuguese side Academica edged through by winning their home legs, while AS Roma and PSV both won their legs 1–0 and Roma progressed on the toss of a coin! And some people complain about penalty shoot-outs. . . .

With just eight teams left, City were keen to avoid the big guns of Gornik, Schalke, Levski-Sofia and Roma, while hoping not to have to travel to Turkey again, this time to face Göztepe. The draw was kind and the first leg of the quarter-final was in Portugal against the relatively unknown university side Academica Coimbra. Domestically, the Blues had also reached the League Cup Final and would play West Brom at Wembley just three days after the clash in Portugal. In the league, City were floundering in mid-table so the cup competitions took on extra importance.

The first leg was a tough, bruising encounter with plenty of gamesmanship and physical threat from Academica, but in front of 15,000 fans, City held their nerve to take a priceless 0–0 draw back to Maine Road.

Schalke produced the performance of the night winning 3–1 in Zagreb, while Gornik lost 3–2 in Sofia and Roma beat Göztepe 2–0 in Italy.

Joe Mercer's side flew back into thick fog in the UK and had to land at Birmingham before being bussed to London. The whole country was in the grip of snow and ice and the League Cup Final was in some doubt, especially after the Horse of the Year Show had made mincemeat of the pitch days earlier.

It went ahead and City earned their first trophy of the season, beating the Baggies 2–1 in extra time with a goal from that renowned goal poacher Glyn Pardoe! The Blues were to be pushed to the limit, however, in the return leg against Academica, with the end of normal time still not producing a goal. It had been a dogged display by the Portuguese side but Tony Towers proved to be the hero on the night with a 119th-minute winner to send the Blues into the last four.

Gornik overturned their 3–2 loss to Sofia by winning 2–1 at home and progressing on away goals. Both Schalke and Roma won their ties with two-goal cushions to make up the final four. Whoever City drew, it was going to be tough, but avoiding Roma and Gornik was paramount and the tie against Schalke, who had lost in a game to Shamrock Rovers in the first round, represented a decent chance of making the final.

City withstood fierce pressure in Germany, losing only by a single goal while Roma and Gornik drew 1–1 in Rome. City turned on the style in the home leg in front of a full-house at Maine Road and goals from Neil Young (2), Bell, Lee and Mike Doyle saw them home 5–1, with Schalke becoming the first side in five European ties to score in Moss Side. With the away goal rule not counting in the last four, Roma led 1–0 in Poland and were set for a final showdown with City until legendary striker Włodzimierz Lubański scored a 90th-minute leveller to send the 100,000 crowd into raptures. He scored again three minutes into extra time but the Italians fought back to earn a 2–2 draw and a play-off in Strasbourg. Another 1–1 draw meant the tie had to be settled by the toss of a coin. This time, Roma's luck ran out and Gornik progressed to the final, leaving the Italians crestfallen at their ludicrous exit.

The final, at the Prater Stadium in Austria, was played in front of a paltry 7,968 fans, with the Poles unable to sell many tickets because of visa problems for their supporters and around 7,000 City fans travelling to Vienna to make up the majority of the crowd. Just before kick-off, the heavens opened on the bowl-shaped venue – with no roof! The irony wasn't lost on Joe Corrigan. Nor, for that matter, was it lost on the rest of the City squad that were waiting patiently in the tunnel.

After training on the Austrian pitch a day before the game, coach Malcolm Allison had given the head groundsman a 'back-hander' to water the pitch so that the surface would accommodate City's slick passing and movement. The blue skies, however, would not last – far from it. A deluge of rain started as City left the dressing room and didn't

Franny Lee tucks home a penalty to make it 2–0 v Gornik Zabrze in the 1970 ECWC final.

halt until the final whistle – the Manchester weather had followed the team across Europe – Allison's efforts had been in vain.

'We had all complained that the grass was too long,' recalled Corrigan, who during the 1969/70 season had established himself as City's number one 'keeper.

'Malcolm decided to get around this by giving the groundsman a little something and later, when it started to rain, we just laughed. It was the way Malcolm was.'

Controversially, the FA Cup Final replay between Leeds and Chelsea was held on the same night as the City v Gornik final, which meant that the game, which should have been a source of national pride, lost some of its prestige. Not to the City players or supporters, though. With just a smattering of supporters inside the enormous Prater Stadium, what they lacked numerically, the Blues fans more than made up for vocally. 'They were fantastic,' Corrigan recalled fondly, 'and made it just like a home match for us.'

Mercer's side rewarded those who had made the journey to Austria with an outstanding first-half display which saw them race in to a 2–0 interval lead.

Neil Young netted the opening goal from inside the six-yard box after Franny Lee had had a goal-bound shot blocked. Then, moments before half time, left-winger Young splashed his way through the defence only to have his charge towards goal unceremoniously halted by the Gornik 'keeper, Kostka. The barrel-chested Lee drilled home a penalty to double the lead and give the Blues what proved to be an unassailable advantage.

As expected, a few tense moments followed in the second period, particularly after Mike Doyle had been forced from the action with an ankle injury. Gornik pulled a goal back in the 68th minute through Ozlizio, but City had too much strength and Ian Bowyer, on for Doyle, almost sneaked a third goal late in the game.

Ironically, when the final whistle blew, the rain stopped, too – wild celebrations followed (for the former rather than the latter).

'The only thing I remember about their goal was that it came from a free kick and took a deflection into the path of the player who scored. There was nothing I could do about it,' said Big Joe.

Corrigan went on to make just under 600 appearances for the Blues and won nine England caps. He finds it hard to name one abiding memory of that miserable night in Vienna, which was illuminated by the result. But of that double cup-winning season, he finds it less difficult to pinpoint a recollection.

'It was just brilliant to play in such a good team,' Corrigan said. 'It was a fantastic year, both for myself and the club. I had just broken into City's team and also got into the England Under-23 side.'

City also became only the second English club to have won a domestic trophy and European cup in the same season (Leeds were the first in 1968). City would reach the semi-final of the same competition the following season, losing out to Chelsea and the 'jinx' of no team ever successfully defending their title would continue until the Cup Winners' Cup was scrapped in 1998 – this despite the defending champions reaching the final eight times. City finished tenth in Division One in 1970 and will forever hold the record of the team finishing lowest in their domestic league after winning the Cup Winners' Cup, but when another trophy was paraded in Albert Square in front of thousands of ecstatic Blues, nobody cared about that, or any other statistic.

3   Georgi Best

CITY 3, NEWCASTLE UNITED 3
DATE: 24 FEBRUARY 1996
COMPETITION: PREMIERSHIP
CITY: IMMEL, SUMMERBEE, HILEY, CURLE, SYMONS, LOMAS, BROWN,
CLOUGH, ROSLER, QUINN, KINKLADZE
ATTENDANCE: 31,115

Where was the author? Watching in the Kippax Stand.

Kevin Keegan's Newcastle United – dubbed 'The Entertainers' by the media – rolled into Maine Road with most of the nation willing them to keep winning games in order to stay ahead of Manchester United in the race for the Premiership title. In the build-up to the game, United supporters, predictably, claimed that the Blues would roll over and die so to help the Geordies towards the Premiership trophy but, of course, this would be anything but the case, as ensuing events would prove. In fact, history has shown that whenever the Reds need a favour from City, for some reason, the Blues generally come through.

It was a crisp and sunny February afternoon as Alan Ball's men kicked-off a game they were expected to lose on current form. With fourteen defeats from twenty-six league matches to date, plus failing to score in almost half of those games, it's understandable why few of the 31,115 crowd that day could have envisaged the football feast about to unfurl before their eyes.

The Blues were still struggling to recover from their awful start to the season during which they failed to win any of their first eleven Premiership games. In that same period, Newcastle had won all of their games and opened up a huge lead at the top – talk about contrasting fortunes! Yet this match was to prove that – at least on the day –there wasn't a great deal between the two teams. City were robbed of the several key first-teamers including Garry Flitcroft, Peter Beagrie, Richard Edghill, Terry Phelan and Ian Brightwell, through either injury or suspension, and had full-back Scott Hiley making his debut.

It was soon clear from the opening exchanges that City were up for the challenge with Georgi Kinkladze in majestic form. As the two success-starved giants threw gentle jabs at each other, it was City who deservedly took the lead on 16 minutes. Hiley made an impressive run down the wing and cut the ball back to Nigel Clough whose vicious low drive clipped Niall Quinn's heel and the ball spun agonisingly over the stranded Pavel Srnicek. There was a moment's silence and then

Georgi Kinkladze in mesmeric form against Newcastle United in 1996.

a deafening roar as the ball nestled in the back of the net sending the packed Maine Road wild with delight.

Kinkladze was masterful, displaying his vast array of skills to an adoring public. The Magpies could do little to stop him in this mood. Yet, despite their dominance, City failed to add to their lead and paid the price on 44 minutes when Belgian centre-half Philippe Albert volleyed home a cracking drive from 10 yards.

The second half was 15 minutes old when the battle between the volatile Faustino Asprilla and City skipper Keith Curle finally boiled over. Asprilla's blatant elbow caught Curle full in the face but the referee either didn't see it or buckled under pressure and ignored it. Two minutes later, justice was seen to be done. Kinkladze was at the heart of City's second on 62 minutes as he weaved in, out and mesmerised the visitors' defence before whipping in a low shot that Srnicek did well to keep out. Kinky gathered the rebound and chipped the ball perfectly to the far post for Quinn to gleefully head home his fifth of the season and second of the game.

City tried to kill the game off with a quick third, but the irrepressible Newcastle were soon back on level terms. Albert, giving a masterful exhibition of attacking defence, pinged in a low cross-shot that Eike Immel could only parry allowing Asprilla – who should have been enjoying an early bath – to screw the ball home from a tight angle for 2–2. It was a bitter pill for the players and fans to swallow.

Back came City again. Steve Lomas crossed from the right wing and Uwe Rosler steered home his sixth of the campaign with only 14 minutes to go and Maine Road once more erupted. Depressingly, it would be the only time that season that the Blues managed to score more than two goals. The defensive frailties that had haunted Ball's team all season would soon rear their ugly head again and just five minutes later it was 3–3. Newcastle's man-of-the-match Albert drilled in a low drive which deflected off Quinn and into the net for his second of the game.

Both teams had chances to win the game, but overall, a draw was a fair result on a day when Kinkladze and Albert lifted those assembled, if only briefly, to a higher plain.

4　Mud and Guts

CITY 2, WEST BROMWICH ALBION 1
DATE: 7 MARCH 1970
COMPETITION: LEAGUE CUP FINAL
CITY: CORRIGAN, BOOK, MANN, DOYLE, BOOTH, OAKES, HESLOP, BELL,
SUMMERBEE (BOWYER), LEE, PARDOE
ATTENDANCE: 97,963

*Where was the author? Probably playing on my three-wheeler bike,
Herbie.*

City's first ever League Cup Final win was played on a muddy, snowy Wembley turf famously described by manager Joe Mercer as 'a pig of a pitch' – a far cry from the superb playing surface everybody had come to expect of England's home stadium. The problem was that – incredibly – the Horse of the Year Show had been held at Wembley just days earlier – unthinkable in today's world where television and football are king.

However, referee James passed the game fit to play, after fans of both teams had earlier volunteered to help clear the snow and probably saved the match from postponement. This was to be a tough game for City – playing in their change red and black striped kit – not only because West Brom were obviously a good side, but because three days before, City had ground out a 0–0 draw in the European Cup Winners' Cup quarter-final away to Portuguese outfit Academica Coimbra. Only the injured Neil Young was missing from the team that ran out to face the Baggies.

City were soon on the rack and fell behind to a Jeff Astle header on six minutes, but it only served to be the wake-up call the Blues needed. Slowly, City began to stifle Albion with Heslop and Booth giving little away at the back and the inspirational Alan Oakes and Mike Doyle surging forward at every opportunity. Try as they might, there would be no further scoring in the first half.

Albion finally managed to create another opportunity as Colin Suggett broke clear, but he made a hash of the chance and was left to rue what might have been. Soon after, on the hour City won a corner. Mike Summerbee flicked on the corner to Colin Bell who cushioned a header into Doyle's path. His first-time shot beat Osborne and City, at last, were level. From then on, it was anybody's game. Summerbee had to be substituted after sustaining a hairline fracture of his leg and when a very young Asa Hartford, who was playing for West Brom, was substituted, his replacement, Krzywicki used his pace to almost grab a winner for the

The 'pig of a pitch' Joe Mercer described prior to the 1970 League Cup final.

Black Country outfit. Later, Franny Lee went close for City, but it wasn't to be and the game went into extra time.

The sapping pitch, the tiring journey from Portugal and extra time combined still couldn't keep this never-say-die City side down and when the watching nation may well have expected West Brom to finish the job off in extra time with their fresher legs, the Blues conjured up a 102nd-minute winner.

Lee chipped a ball to Bell and his back flick fell perfectly for Glyn Pardoe. He looked up, shot and squeezed a drive past the Baggies 'keeper from the corner of the box for a dramatic winner. There were no further goals and Tony Book lifted the trophy for the first time in City's history. It was also the first time the cup had come back to the North-West and – more significantly – it was the very first time the entire 92 clubs of the Football League had taken part. Quite an achievement.

5 'We've Only Got 10 Men!'

TOTTENHAM HOTSPUR 3, CITY 4
DATE: 4 FEBRUARY 2004
COMPETITION: FA CUP 4TH ROUND REPLAY
CITY: ARASON, SUN, TARNAT, DISTIN, DUNNE, BOSVELT,
WRIGHT-PHILLIPS, BARTON, SINCLAIR (MCMANAMAN 80), ANELKA
(MACKEN 27), FOWLER (SIBIERSKI 80)
ATTENDANCE: 30,400

Where was the author? Dancing round the front room with my three-year old son.

It was a match that was, quite simply, unforgettable. For many, it was quintessential Kevin Keegan, with goals, drama, excitement and controversy in almost equal measure and a night that seemed to have sunk City fans' hearts to the deepest pits of despair, ended with scenes of disbelief, elation and ecstasy.

The odds were stacked against the Blues, following a disastrous run of just one win in eighteen. The Keegan magic had faded to a dull lustre and he seemed no longer capable of rallying his badly misfiring team. They needed a boost from somewhere – anywhere – before the damage became irreversible, though after the first 45 minutes of this match at White Hart Lane, it looked like the former England manager might be on the verge of holding his hands up and passing the reins on to somebody else.

For many, the first clash between these two sides at the City of Manchester Stadium had offered the Blues the best opportunity of progressing into the fifth round. A 1–1 draw suggested that chance had passed and within only two minutes of the replay in North London, City faced a monumental challenge as Ledley King showed a sleight of foot not usually associated with central defenders as he cut inside Jihai Sun and fired a spectacular shot past Arnie Arason into the roof of the net.

There was worse to come for City, too. Robbie Keane latched on to a superb through-ball on 19 minutes, controlling the pass and then lifting the ball over Arason to make it 2–0 and then, to compound the agony, Nicolas Anelka limped off with just 27 minutes played – surely the Blues' night couldn't get any worse? As it happened, it could.

Joey Barton's over-the-top challenge on Michael Brown a couple of minutes before the break earned him a yellow card and from the resulting free-kick Christian Ziege curled a beautiful shot into the top corner to put the hosts – it appeared – into the next round.

David James – his absence during the epic 4–3 FA Cup win at Spurs allowed Arnie Arason a rare start. (© Kevin Cummins)

The whistle blew for half-time but Rob Styles' work wasn't over as Barton continued to argue about his booking. Despite warnings from the referee, he persisted and was shown the red card as the rest of the team made their way down the tunnel. Down to ten men, 3–0 down and playing terribly – no wonder Keegan's hair had gone grey so quickly.

Damage limitation seemed the order of the day. Spurs looked set for a cricket score and a five- or six-goal thrashing could spell the end for the Blues' enigmatic manager. But something strange happened. City came out and began to play football and it seemed to take Spurs by surprise. If fortune really did favour the brave, the Blues were going to have to dig deep within their reserves of courage and derring-do if they were to salvage a little pride. When a free-kick was awarded 40 yards out just three minutes after the break, a chance to repair some of the damage presented itself. The excellent Michael Tarnat floated the ball towards the six-yard box where Spurs, perhaps too cocksure, allowed a galloping

Sylvain Distin enough space to fashion a header – of sorts – past Kasey Keller to make it 3–1.

Not long afterwards, Spurs came within a whisker of making it 4–1 as Ziege fired in another superb free-kick, only to see it strike the bar and Keane miss the chance to head home the rebound as Arason scrambled back to stop the ball on the line. Arason, making his debut for City, was immense and would make another two incredible saves to keep the hosts at bay. With almost 70 minutes gone, City were still clinging on 3–1 down. As the ball was cleared by the Spurs defence, Paul Bosvelt hit a low drive that spun wickedly off Anthony Gardner and past Keller to make it 3–2. Suddenly the White Hart Lane crowd were anxious and the players responded accordingly, misplacing passes and looking increasingly nervous.

The 1,500 or so City fans who had made the journey south roared on their ten-man team and, with 10 minutes to go, Shaun Wright-Phillips was put clear through and as Keller raced off his line, he lifted the ball gently past him to make it 3–3. It was a fantastic comeback and even if Spurs had grabbed a winner, proved the team were capable of much better things, but there was still one more twist to come.

With the clock ticking past 90 minutes, City pressed for an unlikely winner. Extra time beckoned and for the home team, a chance to regroup and restore sanity. The ball was deep in the Spurs half when it found its way to Tarnat. The cultured German lifted the ball towards the back post where Jon Macken leapt up, made a terrific connection and then watched as the ball sailed past Keller and into the net – cue pandemonium.

The City fans, players and management went wild and the Tottenham players looked at each other in total disbelief. How could they have thrown it away? Three goals up, 45 minutes to play and the opposition down to ten men. It was scarcely believable.

The whistle went moments later, completing one of the greatest comebacks of all time and one of the most exciting FA Cup matches ever. As Keegan succinctly pointed out afterwards, 'They'll be talking about this match long after we've all gone.' Fortunately, most of us are still here Kev, but we are, indeed, still talking about it.

6 The First Noel

CITY 5, NEWCASTLE UNITED 1
DATE: 18 JANUARY 1975
COMPETITION: DIVISION ONE
CITY: CORRIGAN, HAMMOND, DONACHIE, DOYLE, BOOTH, OAKES,
BELL, SUMMERBEE, MARSH, TUEART, ROYLE
ATTENDANCE: 32,021

Where was the author? Still waiting for someone to take me to my first match . . .

As a seven-year-old Noel Gallagher trundled into Maine Road for the first time with his dad, the Blues were preparing for a home game with Newcastle United who had won an FA Cup tie 2–0 on the same ground just a fortnight earlier. Add to that a 2–1 defeat at St James' Park just six weeks before and Tony Book's side had all the motivation they needed to put the Magpies to the sword.

When Book's side had clicked during the 1974/5 campaign, they did so with conviction and style. In fact, they'd begun the season with a 4–0 win over West Ham and were the early pace-setters in the top flight before enduring a few hiccups and a miserable festive period that included losses to Liverpool and Derby County.

The Blues were very much a team in transition with Franny Lee sold and Mike Summerbee now on the transfer list. Book was carefully assembling his own team from the ashes of the Joe Mercer and Malcolm Allison era, so there were bound to blips along the way. Out of both cup competitions and seemingly out of the title race, it was the Blues' away form that was pegging them back in the League with just one win on the road in thirteen games – more like relegation form than a club challenging for a UEFA Cup spot. At Maine Road, however, City were practically invincible and had won ten, drawn two and lost just one of their thirteen matches.

A disappointing crowd of 32,021 were, nonetheless, hopeful of another home win and Book knew if he could solve the puzzle of his team's away day blues, City could still put in a late challenge for the title. Asa Hartford and Keith MacRae were both missing through injury, meaning recalls for the transfer-listed Summerbee and Joe Corrigan.

The game began at a lively pace with both teams eager to get back to winning ways after recent set-backs. Newcastle had conceded five goals in their last game while City had played out a drab 1–1 draw away to Sheffield United, so the first goal was always going to be vital

Dennis Tueart terrorises the Newcastle defence in January 1975.

and thankfully, it was Geoff Hammond who stabbed the ball home to give City the lead with just seven minutes played.

However, the Magpies roared back into the game with a Malcolm Macdonald thunderbolt levelling the score on 14 minutes. The match continued to ebb and flow with chances at both ends, but it was a boyhood Newcastle United fan, Dennis Tueart, who restored City's lead on 37 minutes, tucking home a penalty kick for his seventh league goal of the season. The Blues went into the break 2–1 up and the second half deteriorated into a feisty affair, particularly after Tueart made it 3–1 six minutes after the restart. Summerbee clashed with Pat Howard and Rodney Marsh aimed a punch at Mickey Burns that referee Ron Challis decided to ignore as tempers boiled over.

City managed to keep their focus and the hapless Geordies were finally put to bed when the brilliant Tueart completed his hat-trick on 84 minutes – his first for the club, though several more would follow. Colin Bell rubbed salt in the visitors' wounds when he added a fifth just two minutes from time to complete an emphatic victory for Book's men and leave the seven-year-old Noel Gallagher smitten for life.

Ironically, the rotten away form continued until the end of the season while the home form went from strength to strength – sixteen wins from twenty-one – resulting in an eighth-place finish – just seven points behind champions Derby County, managed by a certain Brian Clough. Had just four away defeats been victories instead, Book might have been lauded as the best young manager in England instead of Old Big 'Ead.

7   The Trautmann Final

BIRMINGHAM CITY 1, CITY 3
DATE: 5 MAY 1956
COMPETITION: FA CUP FINAL
CITY: TRAUTMANN, LEIVERS, LITTLE, BARNES, EWING, PAUL, JOHNSTONE,
HAYES, REVIE, DYSON, CLARKE
ATTENDANCE: 100,000

Where was the author? Not born yet!

A talented City side returned to Wembley after losing in the final to Newcastle 12 months earlier. After defeat to the Magpies, inspirational captain Roy Paul vowed to return the next year and lift the trophy for the Blues. Remarkably this wasn't a first because Sam Cowan had made the same promise after City lost to Everton in the 1933 FA Cup Final – and then returned to Wembley to beat Portsmouth in 1934.

City manager Les McDowall had assembled a fantastic team with the likes of Bert Trautmann, Roy Little, Ken Barnes, Dave Ewing and Roy Paul – possibly one of the Blues' greatest-ever defences – among its number. With Bobby Johnstone, Joe Hayes, Don Revie and Roy Clarke in attack, it was surprising that City finished only in fourth place in Division One – the cup exploits had undoubtedly diluted the championship challenge.

The route to Wembley had been a perilous one beginning in front of 42,517 at Maine Road and a narrow 2–1 victory over Blackpool with goals from Johnstone and Dyson. A trip to Roots Hall proved equally tough in the fourth round with Joe Hayes scoring the only goal in front of 29,500 people. An amazing 70,640 crammed into Maine Road to see the Blues and Liverpool battle out a 0–0 draw in the fifth round, but City won the replay 2–1 at Anfield in front of nearly 58,000 with Hayes and Dyson grabbing the goals. City then saw off Everton in the quarter-finals with goals from Hayes and Johnstone giving the Blues a 2–1 win in front of 76,129 Maine Road fans as cup fever gripped the blue half of Manchester.

By now seemingly unstoppable, City powered past Spurs at Villa Park in the semi-final with Johnstone scoring the only goal on the day in front of just under 70,000, meaning that skipper Paul's promise had been kept. City were once again at the Twin Towers and were in no mood to play the role of bridesmaid. Only Billy Spurdle was missing from the side that had beaten Spurs as City walked onto the Wembley turf with Birmingham City – a side the Blues had lost 4–3 to at St Andrew's and drawn 1–1

Roy Paul leads City out to face Birmingham in the 1956 FA Cup final.

with in the league already that season. In fact, the Brummies had been drawn away in all four rounds and had more than earned their place in the final having seen off Torquay, West Brom, Leyton Orient, Arsenal and then Sunderland in the semis.

Revie replaced the unfortunate Spurdle and would prove to be far more than just an adequate replacement. City had adopted what would be later known as the 'Revie plan' whereby the traditional no. 9 centre forward played in a deep role behind two other strikers, making it difficult for centre-halves pick him up – a plan based on the successful Hungarian national side (and also much-criticised the previous year in defeat to Newcastle.) This time, however, it would work a treat and the innovative Blues reaped their reward.

Revie played an integral part in what was to be the perfect start for McDowall's team. His 40-yard pass found Roy Clarke who returned the ball to Revie, who then skilfully flicked it into the path of Joe Hayes who slotted home the ball with only three minutes on the clock.

Stunned, Birmingham composed themselves and equalised on 15 minutes through Noel Kinsey and that proved the end of the scoring for the first half. The key to the Blues' triumph came midway through the second half when Dyson was put clear after tremendous work by Revie, Johnstone and Barnes and he made no mistake to restore City's lead. Two minutes later and the famous old trophy was as good as on its way to Maine Road as Johnstone scored his fourth of the competition to make it 3–1 and send the travelling Mancunians into raptures.

The match, however, will always be best remembered for one man's truly incredible bravery. Bert Trautmann, City's legendary former German goalkeeper, fearlessly saved at Murphy's feet 15 minutes from time and took a blow to the neck from the Birmingham striker's knee. Trautmann, clearly in a great deal of pain, continued to play, despite appearing to have sustained a serious injury. The courage he showed in those final minutes took on the stuff of legend when it was later discovered that the big goalkeeper had broken two bones in his neck and a further knock could have left him in a wheelchair – or worse – for the rest of his days. It was an incredible act of heroism as there were no substitute 'keepers on the bench in those days and the reason the 1956 final will always be remembered as Trautmann's final.

8 A Perfect 10

City 10, Huddersfield Town 1
Date: 7 November 1987
Competition: Division Two
City: Nixon, Gidman, Hinchcliffe, Clements, Lake, Redmond, White, McNab, Stewart, Adcock, Simpson
Attendance: 19,583

Where was the author? On the Kippax with my mate Darren Carline.

Those lucky enough to have been at Maine Road on a dismal November afternoon back in 1987 were rewarded with a match they could later deservedly brag 'I was there!' with a smug smile on their faces. The 19,000 or so City fans in the ground that day seem to have become more like 50,000 if the amount of people claiming to have been present is to be believed – there are just too many embarrassed to admit they didn't much fancy a mundane-looking clash with bottom-of-the-table Huddersfield Town.

Malcolm Macdonald was the new boss of the Terriers and his side ran out with high hopes of adding to City's miserable start to the season following relegation from the First Division. The Blues had managed just six wins out of sixteen and sat uncomfortably in mid-table, unable to shake off the hangover of previous campaign's inadequacy.

Huddersfield's kit on the day was a truly awful black and yellow chequered design that was just begging to be thrashed. City had little choice but to do the decent thing – and for once, duly obliged. For the first ten minutes, the Blues were on the rack and could have been 3–0 down, but it soon became clear it wasn't going to be Huddersfield's day.

When a questionable penalty was awarded in the 13th minute, Neil McNab slotted the ball past Cox to put City 1–0 up. From then on, Town capitulated and everything City tried came off. Paul Simpson was in fantastic form and he helped supply Paul Stewart, Tony Adcock and David White to give Mel Machin's side a handsome 4–0 lead at the break. It's often the case that a side leading so convincingly at half time tends to take their foot off the gas in the second period, but it didn't happen on this occasion. Adcock added a fifth on 52 minutes and Stewart scored his second on 66. Adcock became the first player to complete his treble a minute later to make it 7–0 and Stewart made it 8–0 – uncannily – on 80 minutes. There was a hunger among the players and supporters that something unique was happening and the opportunity to reach double figures now acted as further incentive to further punish Huddersfield.

David White sends Maine Road wild by slamming home City's tenth goal against Huddersfield in 1987.

Step forward David White!

White made it 9–0 with five minutes left – could they do it? The excitement was incredible, but the tenth goal of the game went to Huddersfield who scored in the 88th minute when former Blue Andy May scored a penalty. Cue wild, ironic celebrations from the small band of travelling fans. Was there still time to grab goal no. 10? As a ball was lobbed up front it was flicked into White's path and he was clear on goal. With his electric pace he raced toward goal, rounded the 'keeper and planted the ball in the net.

Maine Road went crazy and then the final whistle blew seconds later. Malcolm Macdonald was almost too shell-shocked to speak afterwards, but he would have the last laugh as – typically – Huddersfield won the return 1–0! Only City!

9 The Ballet on Ice

CITY 4, TOTTENHAM HOTSPUR 1
DATE: 9 DECEMBER 1967
COMPETITION: DIVISION ONE
CITY: MULHEARN, BOOK, PARDOE, DOYLE, HESLOP, OAKES, LEE, BELL, SUMMERBEE, YOUNG, COLEMAN
ATT: 35,792

Where was the author? In my cot asleep, I expect.

City's performance against Spurs on a wintry, snow-covered Maine Road pitch back in 1967 epitomised all that was great about Joe Mercer's all-conquering side. Steaming their way towards the league title, the Blues were irrepressible against the North Londoners and made a mockery of the icy, slippery conditions with a display of grace, skill and attacking football at its very best.

The match was actually in some doubt right up until kick-off and could have been called-off, but thankfully it wasn't, and the 35,000 City fans were treated to a game that would go down in club folklore. It was a talented Tottenham side, with four future managers in their side, who drew first blood with the lethal Jimmy Greaves putting the visitors into a 7th-minute lead. The prolific striker followed a Terry Venables free kick from the edge of the box and with his poacher's instinct, found himself on the edge of the six-yard box with the ball at his feet where he then comfortably placed the ball past Ken Mulhearn for a surprise lead. City, however, were in no mood to roll over.

With the snow falling heavily, the Blues launched an attack featuring Mike Doyle, Franny Lee and Tony Coleman. Coleman's cross caused a goalmouth scramble and Mullery deflected the ball to Colin Bell, who smashed the ball home from 18 yards out for a deserved equaliser. Shortly after, Mike Summerbee sent in a cross to the edge of the box and Neil Young's stinging volley was well saved by a young Pat Jennings, the last real action of note in an entertaining first half.

Top scorer Young, having a superb game, must have thought he wasn't destined to get on the score sheet when he sent another shot crashing in from 30 yards out. This time, the ball smacked the bar and bounced to safety. Young then found Summerbee with a perfect cross and the right-winger rose between two defenders to head the ball past Jennings and put the Blues ahead for the first time in the match.

From that point on, Spurs never stood a chance. With City in majestic flow, the visitors had no answer to the constant waves of attack. In the 64th

*Neil Young, graceful on grass or
snow and ice, in 1967.*

minute, the Blues increased
their lead with a move that
started with 'keeper Mulhearn
and never once touched a Spurs
player. Tony Book found Lee,
who fed the ball to Summerbee
just inside the Tottenham half.
Lee scampered down the flank
to receive Summerbee's clever
return ball and whipped a
wicked cross-shot that hit the
foot of the post. The enigmatic
Coleman was following up and
was presented with the easiest
of chances to volley the ball
into the back of the net and
virtually seal the points.

Dispirited, Spurs fell yet
further adrift. Bell's shot was
parried by Jennings and the
ball fell to Young who finally
scored the goal his all-round play richly deserved. Both Young and
Coleman hit the post with successive shots as the Blues attempted to
pile the misery on for Tottenham but there was to be no more scoring.
The ballet on ice was over and the secret of City's sure-footedness was
later revealed by skipper Book who advised his team-mates to unscrew
their studs to leave just the tips of a metal thread showing, effectively
making the boots perfect to grip the ice and snow. That proved to be
the difference on the day and as the Londoners skidded, slipped and
tumbled, City played the ball around as though there wasn't a snowflake
in sight.

10   The Power and the Glory

CITY 1, IPSWICH TOWN 0
DATE: 11 APRIL 1981
COMPETITION: FA CUP SEMI-FINAL (AT VILLA PARK)
CITY: CORRIGAN, RANSON, McDONALD, REID, POWER, CATON,
BENNETT, GOW, MACKENZIE, HUTCHISON, REEVES SUB: BOOTH
ATTENDANCE: 46,537

Where was the author? In the seats opposite the Holte End with my cousin Don Roberts, having had our standing tickets stolen on the way to Villa Park.

The dramatic FA Cup semi-final victory over Ipswich Town is still an all-time favourite game for many City supporters. In fact, most prefer the memory of the fantastic win at Villa Park to the final itself. It was an amazing day for the Blues, but it could have been very different had Ipswich taken any of the early opportunities presented to them.

With half of the Holte End comprised of City fans and half of Ipswich, the game kicked-off at 3.00 p.m. on an overcast Saturday afternoon – back when semi-finals used to be played on Saturday afternoons – and the East Anglians were soon on the attack. Bobby Robson's Ipswich side was packed with quality, grace, talent . . . and Alan Brazil – and were riding high in the First Division table while John Bond's team had recovered from being relegation favourites to a comfortable mid-table position with formidable cup form.

The Suffolk outfit had eight full internationals – four England, two Dutch and two Scottish – compared to City's lone (occasional) England international Joe Corrigan. Current form for both sides suggested a tight encounter, but City struggled in the early minutes and the graceful Arnold Mühren presented Brazil with a sitter on 11 minutes but he contrived to miss the ball completely. Shame!

Tommy Hutchison then cleared a thunderous Kevin Beattie header off the line four minutes later as the Blues, playing in red and black stripes, grimly hung on. City began to battle back inspired by Gerry Gow who informed Franz Thijssen of his presence with a crunching challenge that earned him a talking-to from referee Pat Partridge.

Eric Gates, he of the toothless grin, blasted the ball over from close range as Ipswich continued to spurn chances. Dave Bennett was scythed down by Beattie towards the break and Gow's vicious drive was gathered at the second attempt by future City goalkeeper Paul Cooper. The teams went into the break locked at 0–0 with the Blues slowly beginning to ask a few questions themselves and it was the three musketeers – Gow, Hutchison and McDonald who were causing Town most problems.

Brazil missed yet another golden opportunity after the break and the dangerous Beattie, a constant threat from set pieces, almost put his side ahead on the hour with a header that went inches past the post. The City defence were responding magnificently to the pressure with Tommy Caton in particular in outstanding form. Beattie again sent a header inches over and the burly Ipswich defender must have guessed by that point it wasn't going to be their day by this time.

City skipper Paul Power, scorer of a magnificent free kick against Ipswich Town during the 1981 FA Cup semi-final at Villa Park.

A mid-air collision between Beattie and Bennett, minutes from time, saw the Ipswich man limp off and McCall come on as a replacement as fatigue began to take over. The referee finally blew for the end of ninety minutes and both teams took a much-needed breather before the extra time began.

City attacked the Holte End for the first period, and with exactly 100 minutes on the clock, were awarded a free kick on the edge of the Ipswich box. Skipper Paul Power, who had scored in every round bar one, sized up the defensive wall and Steve Mackenzie rolled the ball gently into his path. The crowd held its breath as he whipped a curling shot towards the goal. Cooper scrambled across to his right but the ball sailed into the top left-hand corner of the net. Half the ground erupted and the blue masses behind the goal went wild.

City were on their way to the FA Cup Final for the first time since 1969 with a wonderful goal scored in the 100th minute of the 100th year of FA Cup football. Surely fate was playing a hand in the competition . . . or was it?

The celebrations continued for several minutes, but there were still 20 minutes to play. Yet there was a feeling that the game was as good as over. Flags, scarves and banners were raised as the City fans saluted their heroes and despite a few close calls, Ipswich looked totally demoralised and the scenes and noise that greeted the final whistle will live long in the memory of those who were there. City supporters may not have had too many chances to celebrate over the past thirty years, but when they do, they party with the best of them. As it turned out, it wasn't City's year after all, despite being ahead in the final and the subsequent replay, it was Spurs who lifted the trophy in the Centenary Cup Final, not the Blues.

11   Learning Latin

CITY 1, JUVENTUS 0
DATE: 15 SEPTEMBER 1976
COMPETITION: UEFA CUP 1ST ROUND, 1ST LEG
CITY: CORRIGAN, DOCHERTY, DONACHIE, DOYLE, WATSON, CONWAY,
BARNES (POWER), KIDD, ROYLE, HARTFORD, TUEART
ATTENDANCE: 36,955

Where was the author? Listening to Brian Clarke's commentary.

City's 'reward' for winning the League Cup seven months before was drawing the pre-tournament favourites in the opening round of the UEFA Cup. The Blues had returned to Europe after an absence of four years for the start of the 1976/7 season where they faced the might of Juventus who, although being one of the greatest names in world football, were, surprisingly, still without a European trophy having lost the European Cup Final in 1973.

City, on the other hand, had brought home the European Cup Winners' Cup six years earlier and also finished semi-finalists in the same competition the following season. It was a huge game for Juve as well as City. As a gauge of how strong the Serie A outfit were at this point, it's worth noting that many of the Juve side went on to form the backbone of Italy's 1982 World Cup-winning side. Goalkeeping legend Dino Zoff, Antonio Cabrini and Claudio Gentile made a formidable defensive trio while Marco Tardelli graced their midfield. The Juventus manager that night may have a familiar ring – Giovanni Trapattoni, Italy's World Cup manager for Japan/Korea 2002 and currently the boss of the Republic of Ireland.

The general feeling prior to this match was that the Blues would need a minimum two-goal lead to take to Turin, because anything else against a team renowned for getting the job done on their own patch, would likely see Tony Book's side exit stage left. The Blues had done their homework, but everything would hinge on the ability to take their chances – likely to be few and far between – when presented.

Juventus allowed City plenty of possession on the night and were quite happy to try to hit the Blues on the break. On the occasions when City did penetrate the Italians' back four, international Zoff showed why he was perhaps the best in the world at the time by producing two world-class saves – one in particular, from Brian Kidd, was not dissimilar to Gordon Banks' wondrous one-handed stop against Pelé in 1970. He also somehow tipped a Dennis Tueart effort onto the crossbar as City gave a fantastic account of themselves. Tueart, Kidd, Peter Barnes and Joe Royle caused the Italians headaches all night and the forwards' collective reward came from the head of Kidd when, after 44 minutes, the former Manchester United striker sent a firm header past Zoff following Tueart's corner and Royle's flick-on.

Suddenly, the Italians' mask slipped and the visitors resorted to some cynical challenges aimed at stopping the Blues increasing their advantage. Barnes, always a threat, limped out of the game on the hour after several crunching tackles that probably would have earned red cards each time in today's game. Asa Hartford was outstanding and, had the injured Colin Bell been available, City might have put the game out of Juventus' reach.

After the game, Book said, 'I don't say we will win in Italy, but we will do enough to qualify for the next round.' As it turned out, the fear that one goal wasn't going to be enough was confirmed when Juventus went 2–0 ahead in the return and promptly shut up shop until the final whistle. The Turin side then completed a Manchester double, beating United in the second round 3–0 in the return leg, having lost the first leg at Old Trafford 1–0. They then saw off Shakhtar Donetsk 3–1 on aggregate in the third round before eliminating FC Magdeburg, AEK Athens and, finally, winning the competition by beating Atletico Bilbao on the away goals rule after a two-legged final.

Brian Kidd, scorer of the Blues'
winning goal against Juventus in
1976.

12   Reign in Spain

ATLETICO BILBAO 3, CITY 3
DATE: 17 SEPTEMBER 1969
COMPETITION: EUROPEAN CUP WINNERS' CUP, ROUND ONE, 1ST LEG
CITY: CORRIGAN, BOOK, PARDOE, DOYLE, BOOTH, OAKES, SUMMERBEE,
BELL, YOUNG, LEE, BOWYER
ATTENDANCE: 45,000

Where was the author? Probably asleep with a Farley's Rusk not too far away.

Having been unceremoniously dumped out of the European Cup in the first round the previous season, City approached their next foray into European competition with a far more relaxed, almost gung-ho attitude, concentrating on their attacking strengths instead of locking defensive horns with their opponents and ultimately paying a heavy price.

The Blues had been drawn away to Atletico Bilbao for the first leg and came into the match on the back of a stunning 3–0 league win away to Tottenham Hotspur. But things didn't go too smoothly for Joe Mercer's men – and this was even before they left Manchester Airport. The first problem was an infuriating five-hour delay as the plane, a Comet jet, was withdrawn from service with technical problems. The relief plane from London then had to have its wheels changed after the captain decided they were unfit for further use.

To make matters worse, Tommy Booth became ill and was diagnosed with tonsillitis shortly before the flight, making him doubtful for the game. The team finally made the journey to Spain but on arrival, the coach sent to collect them sent Malcolm Allison into a rage. The vehicle was filthy and someone had been sick on one of the seats.

The Blues arrived at their hotel, checked-in and then prepared for a training session some 8 miles away. The coach driver who had taken them to the hotel refused to drive them anywhere else and another bus had to be ordered, but that was in an even worse condition. Allison ordered a fleet of taxis instead and raged:

> I had heard of these sort of tactics before in Europe but I never really expected it to happen here. But then perhaps I should have known after the way Joe Mercer and myself were treated when we went to watch Bilbao in San Sebastian recently. We were given seats for the match behind a goal with a great pillar in our way. I was determined not to put up with that, for

there were plenty of seats available in the main stand. But even then it was only because officials of Zagreb, Bilbao's opponents, gave up their seats for us that we were able to get a decent view of the game. At the time I thought nothing of that, but now after the latest incident I know better. But I can assure you we will get our own back tonight.

Mercer was his usual calm self as his side prepared for the game. He refused to allow the dirty tricks to upset his plans: 'We'll tackle the Spaniards in the same we took Spurs on their own ground – and you know what happened there.'

The Blues had crushed Tottenham by playing a skilful brand of defensive football in their opponents' half and Mercer was delighted with the way his side had performed. 'I have maintained in the past that we needed to be tighter at the back, but I didn't mean we were going to stick nine or ten men in front of the goalkeeper,' said Joe. 'Any fool can build a defensive wall like that provided the players are stupid enough to stand for it. The way I look at is that if you are going to build a wall at all, build it on the halfway line. As soon as you lose the ball you are playing defensive football because then you have to get it back.'

With the City side pumped up and ready to exact their own brand of revenge, the Spaniards began systematically taking the Blues apart from the off and it looked as though there may be a mountain to climb in the return at Maine Road.

Joe Corrigan, a young and relatively inexperienced goalkeeper at the time, seemed to let the atmosphere get the better of him and he looked nervous and edgy throughout the game. Booth, who had been passed fit, was slowed by a nasty knock to his ankle and was given the run-around by home forward Arieta.

Bilbao's incessant pressure paid off when, after just nine minutes, Agioitia made it 1–0. City were still punch-drunk when Clemente made it 2–0 not long after, but refused to buckle and where many sides would have been engulfed by the slick Spaniards, the Blues dug in and started to play their game. All was not lost and with the hosts unable to maintain the frenetic pace, City clawed a goal back just before half time through Neil Young who rifled a typically powerful drive past Iribar.

Atletico weren't finished and just when it seemed they were flagging slightly, they found their second wind and increased the lead to 3–1 with a goal from Uriarte. To their credit, City, who had the bit between their teeth, continued to concentrate on knocking the ball around and sticking to their game-plan and were rewarded when walking-wounded Booth pulled another goal back with a header from a corner to make it 3–2 – a

Ian Bowyer celebrates Luis Echeberria's own goal against Atletico Bilbao in 1969.

result that most sides would have settled for considering the way things had been going earlier in the match.

This, however, was no ordinary side and with five minutes left, Colin Bell drove forward onto a Tony Book pass, whipped in a low cross and the ball was turned past Iribar by Bilbao defender Echeberria for a dramatic equaliser. The City fans celebrated and it was no more than Mercer's courageous side deserved – it was the result the players needed to give them the belief to progress in the competition.

'The lads are not satisfied. They were a bit niggled at the end because they thought they could have won. But just wait until we play the second leg. We'll play aggressively and really give Bilbao something to think about,' said Allison later.

The Blues were true to his word and won the return at Maine Road 3–0 in front of almost 50,000 fans with goals from Ian Bowyer, Bell and Alan Oakes. With confidence flying high, City went all the way to the final and beat Gornik Zabrze 2–1 in Vienna. Few doubted the path had been cleared by the magnificent comeback in Bilbao.

13   Sticky Toffees

EVERTON 2, CITY 2
DATE: 7 MARCH 1981
COMPETITION: FA CUP 6TH ROUND
CITY: CORRIGAN, RANSON, MCDONALD, REID, POWER, CATON, TUEART,
GOW, MACKENZIE, HUTCHISON, REEVES
ATTENDANCE: 52,791

Where was the author? Listening to Brian Clarke's updates on Piccadilly Radio.

Goodison Park in 1981 was an intimidating place at the best of times, but, as thick grey clouds floated in on off the Mersey and nearly 53,000 fans packed in to see who would edge a step closer to Wembley, it was definitely the place to be. City, resurrected under John Bond's flamboyant leadership, had swept through the early rounds of the FA Cup, dishing out thrashings to Malcolm Allison's Crystal Palace and Bond's old Norwich City side 4–0 and 6–0 respectively, before winning 1–0 in a tight game at Peterborough United in the fifth round.

This then was to be a battle royale with Gordon Lee's Everton with the reward being a place in the last four of England's most prestigious competition – a prospect which would have made Blues fans laugh out loud in October when City were cast adrift at the bottom of the table and in complete disarray.

With the noise deafening and City backed by an estimated 12,000 travelling fans, the two sides tore into each other in the typical death-or-glory style that only the FA Cup can inspire. Everton were lining up with four players who would eventually play for City in the shape of former midfielder Asa Hartford, Steve McMahon, Imre Varadi and John Gidman.

With Hartford and Gow swapping bone-crunching tackles in midfield in the early stages, it was left to Mackenzie and Power to try to make headway for City. However, despite having some reasonable half-chances during an aggressive first half, City went behind just before the break as Peter Eastoe drew first blood for the home side. With the ground shuddering to the Everton fans' celebrations, City were back in it with a rapier thrust just two minutes later. Power's looping centre was headed down by Kevin Reeves and there was Gow, having escaped from Hartford's shackles for a moment, to flick the ball into the net.

Three minutes into the second half, City threw all their good work away when they conceded an unnecessary penalty in front of the baying hordes on the Gwladys Street terrace. Tommy Caton's lumbering challenge on

*Full-back Bobby McDonald's two
goals in two minutes would see
Everton off in the replay of the 1981
FA Cup quarter-final at Maine Road.*

Varadi left the Everton player face down in the mud and referee Peter Willis (an old foe of City's) with no doubts. Trevor Ross made no mistake from the spot, putting the home side back in front at 2–1.

The effort that went into City's second fight-back was breathtaking and bore testament to the belief Bond had driven into his team. With time running out, darkness falling and the pitch cutting up into little more than a quagmire, Bond's battlers surged forward time and again until, in the 84th minute, the Everton defence was finally breached once again.

A classic City build-up down the left saw two separate one-twos played between Reeves and Mackenzie and then Mackenzie and Paul Power. Power, the epitome of that terrific cup run, dug deep to find the energy which carried him on to the edge of the box before scooping a tired right leg at the ball, just as Mick Lyons came thundering in with his challenge. It sailed high over the out-rushing McDonough and seemed to hang for an eternity before dropping into the back of the net. The celebrations began behind the goal in the Park End as Power was swamped by team-mates.

The Sunday papers named it 'abrasive', 'supercharged', 'gruelling', 'livewire' and 'energy-sapping'. It had been all of that and much more. City steamed past Everton in the ensuing replay and Ipswich in the semi-final before ultimately falling unluckily to Spurs at Wembley.

14 Bye, Bye, Fergie?

City 5, Manchester United 1
Date: 23 September 1989
Competition: Division One
City: Cooper, Fleming, Hinchcliffe, Bishop, Gayle, Redmond, White, Morley, Oldfield, Brightwell, Lake
Subs: Beckford, Megson
Att: 43,246

Where was the author? Dancing like an idiot about midway along the Kippax.

It was an afternoon no City fan will ever forget. It was a day when everything went right on the pitch but there would also be a huge price to pay for all the celebrations and taunting by the buoyant Blues faithful. It was to be the last derby win over United for thirteen years, prior to the last-ever Maine Road derby in 2002.

Still, if you are only going to have one win in thirteen years against your deadliest of rivals, it must be done in style and nobody could argue that the Blues didn't do exactly that on a fairly mild September afternoon back in 1989. City, just promoted and back among the nation's elite, began the 111th Manchester derby having won only one match of the new campaign. Four points from eighteen represented an awful start for Mel Machin's men, and United, though not setting the division on fire, had added multi-million pound signings such as Gary Pallister and Paul Ince to their squad and were clear favourites to take all three points.

By comparison, City's entire squad had cost around £2.5 million, but did included six Manchester-born players. Alex Ferguson was relatively new to the Reds and this was his first Manchester derby. Both clubs lost influential players shortly before the kick-off with Neil McNab and Clive Allen missing for City while United's Bryan Robson failed a late fitness test. Respected Bolton referee Neil Midgley blew for kick-off as the deafening noise of more than 43,000 supporters packed into Maine Road reached fever pitch.

It was matters off the pitch, however, that grabbed the crowd's attention early on when fighting broke out in the North Stand. Dozens of United supporters had infiltrated the seats reserved for home support only and the game was held up for eight minutes as police ejected the troublemakers who were led down the side of the pitch having terrorised areas usually filled with families and young kids.

Andy Hinchcliffe (centre), Paul Lake and Ian Brightwell celebrate City's fifth against United in the best Manchester derby . . . ever!

The players re-emerged from the dressing room and restarted the game. It was City who seemed to have drawn impetus from the incident and ten minutes later, went ahead. David White dragged a cross back hopefully into the United box. Pallister was caught flat-footed, and the ball rolled to David Oldfield who buried a rising shot past Jim Leighton and into the roof of the net.

City fans barely had time to stop celebrating the first goal before they were once again dancing on the terraces. Paul Lake scrambled towards the United goal and forced Leighton to parry his shot, but Trevor Morley was first to the loose ball with a brave lunge and toe-poked home the Blues' second goal in the space of a minute. Maine Road went wild. The 2–0 scoreline didn't flatter the Blues either, and they quickly set about attempting to finish the game before half time.

Punch-drunk United couldn't respond and with only one Mancunian in their side, it seemed they didn't have the heart to save themselves. Meanwhile, City poured forward relentlessly. Steve Redmond won the ball in his own half and fed Oldfield down the right-hand flank. Roared on by the Kippax, the former Luton man drove forward and whipped in a perfect cross for new cult hero Ian Bishop to plant the ball past Leighton with a magnificent diving header.

The game was as good as over with just 36 minutes on the clock and the City fans were in dreamland. United looked bewildered and beaten and the half-time whistle was something of a disappointment for the home fans who wanted the action to continue for as long as possible. A display as perfect as the first 45 minutes could only be hindered by a break, and for a while, that was exactly how the second half panned out.

United had more purpose and invention about their play and after 51 minutes, finally pulled a goal back, Russell Beardsmore crossing for future City boss Mark Hughes to volley a typically spectacular and unstoppable drive past Paul Cooper. Danny Wallace then had a fine run and shot minutes later as the game went from joyous to tortuous in the space of a few minutes for the Blues fans.

But this was City's day and, as if reawakened, Machin's side stormed back. Lake again found his way through the visitors' defence and had a shot saved before squaring the rebound to Oldfield who tapped the ball into an empty net for his second and City's fourth. With a 4–1 deficit, United's hopes of a revival were again in shreds and four minutes later, unbridled joy became ecstasy for City with perhaps one of the best derby goals of all-time. The irrepressible Bishop fed White with a measured ball and White crossed first time for Andy Hinchcliffe to power a bullet header past a forlorn Leighton to end the contest with just over an hour gone.

The Kippax taunted Ferguson and the United fans who had tried to leave – only to be rebuffed by stewards – all with just 62 minutes played! The Blues took pity on the Reds and, somehow, 5–1 remained the final score, though nobody was complaining.

City boss Machin said later, 'I was proud of my players. Proud of the way they approached the game and proud of the way they conducted themselves in achieving this splendid result. I thought we'd reached a standard of perfection in the 10–1 demolition of Huddersfield Town a couple of seasons back, but this latest performance surpassed even that and it's left me with a lovely feeling.'

Sentiments echoed by each and every City fan, though just six weeks later, Machin was sacked after a 6–0 defeat at Derby County.

15   To Elland Back

LEEDS UNITED 1, CITY 2
DATE: 7 JANUARY 1978
COMPETITION: FA CUP 3RD ROUND
CITY: CORRIGAN, CLEMENTS, DONACHIE, BOOTH, WATSON, OWEN, BARNES, BELL, KIDD, HARTFORD, TUEART
ATTENDANCE: 38,516

Where was the author? At home having been banned from travelling to 'grounds like Leeds'.

The third round FA Cup tie City played at Elland Road in January 1978 was not only a classic of its kind, but represents a microcosm of all that was '70s football – two star-studded sides, flowing football, flowing hair, heaving terraces, ill-discipline among the players and considerable crowd trouble. Bill Elliot, writing in the *Express*, was moved to say, 'It takes a rare kind of match to overcome pitch invasions, 16 minutes of stoppage and some of the worst crowd behaviour in the history of our football. The fact that there was as much talk about the game on the park as the sickness on the terraces highlights just how special was Manchester City's defeat of Leeds United.'

City's side, containing internationals in almost every position, was fresh from a glorious season where the Blues finished a single point behind the champions Liverpool. That 1976/7 season had also witnessed a great run to the fifth round of the FA Cup where City were more than unfortunate to exit at Leeds, having ably disposed of Newcastle and West Brom, when Trevor Cherry's late toe-poke ended hopes for another year – a year, in fact, when many had felt it was City's turn to lift the famous old trophy. Here then – just under a year later – was an opportunity for the Blues to exact revenge on the Yorkshiremen.

A packed Elland Road witnessed a flowing classic of a match from the very first whistle. With Peter Barnes and Dennis Tueart swapping wings throughout the first half, City took the game to a heavily fancied Leeds side, who had already completed the league double over Tony Book's side by that point. Led by the inspirational Colin Bell, four games into his emotive comeback, Gary Owen and a typical never-say-die performance from Asa Hartford, City were firing on all cylinders in the middle of the park. The first half saw the Leeds rearguard soak up spells of heavy pressure with Tueart heading just wide after great work on the right by Owen and Barnes' jinking run, ending with McQueen upending him for a nailed-on penalty that the referee decided against giving. Such was the visitors' dominance, by the end of the first 45 minutes the Leeds players had taken to fighting among themselves. After a series of City corners threatened to create havoc, team-mates Harvey and McQueen were spoken to by the referee after swinging wild punches at each other. The referee even saw fit to walk to the touchline and warn Leeds manager Jimmy Armfield to get his team under control. This would be a prelude to more serious problems later in the game, as some of the Leeds supporters, buoyed by what they had seen on the pitch, would decide to ape (an apt word on this occasion) their heroes' unprofessional behaviour. Somehow, however, Leeds survived the onslaught to retreat to the shelter of the changing rooms at 0–0.

City's attacks did not let up after the interval, and after McQueen had fouled Brian Kidd on 62 minutes, they got their richly deserved breakthrough. With the City fans packing the terraces behind the goal and all the way down the side of the ground as far as the half-way line, there was a huge upswell of noise as Watson lofted the ball forward, Bell bravely looped the ball on with his head and Tueart flung himself through the bodies to head high past Harvey. As the net bulged, Tueart was treated to a mouthful of turf as Paul Reaney arrived too late and squashed him into the penalty area mud. A mass of sky blue scarves greeted the goal, but City were not finished. Leeds, committed now to chasing the equaliser, were leaving gaps at the back, as the game ebbed and flowed furiously. City's killer second goal came with 18 minutes to go; as Donachie crossed from the left wing, Bell got up above Frank Gray to head powerfully forward, Harvey – mistiming his jump slightly – pushed the ball up onto the bar and, as players rushed in on the loose ball, Barnes got a toe end to it and it was in the back of the net, doubling the Blues' lead. Clarke's rugged challenge on Joe Corrigan just after this earned him a talking-to from the referee, as the atmosphere on the Leeds Kop began to change palpably for the worse. Sure enough, with 13 minutes left on the clock, a massive surge of Leeds fans carried those at the front onto the pitch at the Kop end. With City dominating the home team, this was the home fans' solution – try to get the game abandoned. Referee Seal took the teams off and, to his credit, reappeared with a tiny microphone to tell the supporters, 'This match will not be abandoned.' He repeated his mantra for effect (earning great cheers from the travelling City fans) before the players finally reappeared some 15 minutes later. By now, the game had lost its pattern, the crowd were being held back by police horses and most wanted it to finish as quickly as possible. City continued to press. Tueart had a great chance on the breakaway to make it 3–0, but it was Tony Currie who was bossing things now and he it was who inspired Leeds' mini-comeback, being upended by Corrigan in the box at the end of a weaving run. The penalty was despatched low to Corrigan's left by Frank Gray, to create a tense finale. With the thousands of Blues fans singing their songs of victory, the whistle finally went with the clock past 5.00 p.m. to end an epic day of cup football. The draw for the fourth round was unkind in the extreme – after the valiant effort of beating Leeds on their own turf, City were drawn away to Brian Clough's all-conquering Nottingham Forest and went out to them 2–1 at the City Ground. The memories of the battling and swashbuckling display in Yorkshire would not be dimmed, however.

Joe Corrigan – City's rock throughout the 1970s – played his part in the 2–1 FA Cup third-round win at Leeds in 1978.

16   Wolves at the Door

City 2, Wolverhampton Wanderers 1
Date: 28 December 1981
Competition: Division One
City: Corrigan, Ranson, Wilson, Reid, Bond, Caton, Kinsey,
Reeves, Francis, Hartford, Hutchison
Attendance: 40,298

*Where was the author? In the Main Stand press box where I was allowed
to watch the end of games due to my mum's job.*

Festive programmes have, by and large, been fairly happy times for
City over the years. The Blues often play well around the Christmas
and New Year period when the league games come fast and furious,
and John Bond's team approached Christmas 1981 with a certain amount
of optimism with early December victories over Aston Villa at Maine
Road and Coventry City at Highfield Road elevating the club to seventh
in the First Division table.

It was a remarkable turnaround by City considering that barely more
than a year before they had been marooned at the bottom of the table
with only four points from a possible thirty-three. Bond had performed
miracles to take the club to the Centenary FA Cup Final the previous
May, while steering the team to a comfortable mid-table finish in the
process.

The last game before the holiday period augured well for City – a
home clash with rock bottom Sunderland. A brace from Trevor Francis
had given City a 2–1 lead with minutes remaining, but the Black Cats
somehow clawed their way back with two goals in the dying seconds to
win 3–2. City remained in seventh in what was proving to be the most
open championship for many years.

A daunting Boxing Day trip to Anfield, where City had failed to
win in the league since 1953, hardly inspired confidence after such a
galling defeat to the North-Easterners but, as Britain shivered in freezing
conditions of snow and ice, the Blues gave their supporters a belated
Christmas present in the form a stunning 3–1 victory over Liverpool.

The win pushed City into fourth place and with most of the holiday
programme once again postponed a couple of days later, Maine Road's
under-soil heating presented Bond's men with the chance to top the table.
A holiday crowd of more than 40,000 packed into the ground for the visit
of Wolves who may have been struggling near the foot of the table, but
had enjoyed two wins in their previous four visits to Maine Road. Injury

to Bobby McDonald presented Clive Wilson with his first team debut while another youngster, Steve Kinsey, was making his home bow.

The tension was almost tangible as the match kicked-off. Everyone knew victory would see City top the table and the crowd's nerves seemed to filter through to the players. Wolves began brightly and slowly took command of the match.

The scrappy first period ended 0–0 and Bond led his troops into the dressing room for a dressing down and, as a result, City re-emerged looking more focused and determined not to the let the opportunity of leading the tightly-packed First Division into the New Year pass them by. With only eight minutes of the second half gone, Asa Hartford drilled his second goal in three days to put the Blues 1–0 up.

Wolves, however, were in no mood to ease City's path to the top and thanks to an eagle-eyed linesman, they were presented with a chance of staging a late recovery when Joe Corrigan was adjudged to have stepped outside his area while making a clearance up field. The Wolverhampton players, once again tapping into to the Blues' anxiety and feeling of injustice made the most of the incident as the home side appeared to lose their concentration.

Ray Daniel drove the free-kick low and hard and Corrigan watched in horror as the ball skidded off his hands and into the net for a deserved equaliser. Wolves then lived up to their name and moved in for the kill. City were hanging on with defenders Tommy Caton and Kevin Bond particularly outstanding, but when Wolverhampton striker Mel Eaves claimed his angled shot had crossed the line a few minutes later, Maine Road held its collective breath. Clive Wilson, hugely impressive on his debut, had seemingly managed to scramble the ball to safety and the referee agreed with the linesman that the whole of the ball had not crossed the line, much to the chagrin of the visitors who protested vehemently against the decision.

Though City were still out of sorts, they were still in the game and with five minutes to go, Trevor Francis, largely anonymous throughout the match, showed why City had splashed out more than a million pounds on his undoubted match-winning qualities. Corrigan launched a mighty clearance into the Wolves half and defender George Berry could only direct his header into Francis' path.

Francis took a half-a-dozen steps forward and lashed a thunderous drive into the back of the net from the edge of the box. Maine Road erupted and this time the Blues held out in the final nervous moments to win 2–1. The celebrations at the final whistle were testament enough to how the City fans felt about topping the table for the first time in four years. Bond said later, 'I must have aged four years, although I'd feel

Kevin Reeves formed a decent partnership with Trevor Francis during the 1981/2 campaign – one that saw the Blues top the table at Christmas and finish tenth five months later!

worse if I were the Wolves manager and had lost after playing so well. Trevor Francis will never score another goal like that even if he lives to be 150, but then, that's why he's a million pound player.'

City maintained their challenge at the top for a month, but just three wins in the final seventeen games meant the side that had topped the table going into 1982 had finished a disappointing tenth by the end of the season. The dip in form had been a pre-cursor for the following campaign when City would be relegated on the final day of the season. The goal from Francis and the league table the following day had, at least, given the City fans a warm glow amid freezing conditions.

17   Hammers to Fall

City 4, West Ham United 3
Date: 21 October 1972
Competition: Division One
City: Healey, Book, Donachie, Doyle, Booth, Jeffries, Summerbee,
Bell, Marsh, Lee, Towers
Attendance: 30,890

Where was the author? Most likely playing with my toy cars.

City went into this game with the spectre of an unlikely relegation battle ahead of them. After the glorious era just a few years earlier, the Blues were beginning to struggle to live up to those trophy-laden seasons. They had finished the previous season fourth after seemingly being in sight of the title up until the final few weeks of the campaign.

City had started the new season particularly erratically and even found themselves anchored to the bottom of the table in early September after a defeat to Crystal Palace at Selhurst Park. The team was ageing and personnel changing, as were things behind the scenes. This was the first season without the steadying influence of Joe Mercer, who had been forced out during a boardroom takeover and was now to be found in charge of Coventry, leaving Malcolm Allison with carte blanche to tinker with the team as he wished.

Away from the pitch, Peter Swales was now installed as chairman and a bright new era was supposedly beginning for the Blues. By October they had risen through the ranks slightly and were battling in lower mid-table when they came up against a West Ham side suffering similar problems. Their star-studded side was also beginning to disintegrate, although some, such as Billy Bonds, Bobby Moore and Trevor Brooking still remained. Martin Peters and Geoff Hurst had already been sold on to Spurs and Stoke respectively by this time, but despite this, the Londoners were sitting pretty in the top half of the table by the time they visited Maine Road.

They were, however, still smarting from a shambolic League Cup exit at the hands of Fourth-Division Stockport County and travelled north looking to put that disaster out of their minds. The 30,890 crowd that assembled that October day was not aware of how close they came to seeing City perform without the man who turned out to be the match's catalyst. Colin Bell had spent the whole of the previous week laid low with a stomach bug, but he hauled himself out of bed not only to take part in the game but

Mike Summerbee, on the mark during the 4–3 win over West Ham in 1972.

to run the show completely with a heroic display in what turned out to be an exhilarating match. 'I felt a bit hazy at times,' Bell admitted stoically to the press afterwards, but it hadn't showed as the Blues tore into the East Londoners right from the start. In their previous game, the Blues had been criticised for a lack of cohesion in an embarrassing defeat to Coventry City, where Joe Mercer would have been forgiven a wry smile as his new charges triumphed over the Blues. The passes on this occasion, however, found their targets with unerring accuracy and City's football flowed magnificently as West Ham were swept away in a tide of attacking football.

By half time, City were already cruising at 4–2 up, goals from Tony Towers, Mike Summerbee and two from Rodney Marsh interspersed by a couple from West Ham's Clyde Best and Johnny Ayris. Attack after attack stemmed from the gentle prompting of Bell, as City ran rings around their guests. Showing no signs of the illness that had sidelined him, and ably assisted by the young Towers, Bell ran effortlessly from end to end in constant support of Marsh, Lee and Summerbee in City's attack.

Inevitably, the foot was taken off the accelerator in the second half and City conceded a third goal to England legend Bobby Moore, leaving an unnecessarily edgy finish for the faithful to endure. This game would herald a terrific run in November, which saw City defeat Derby, Manchester United and Everton with an aggregate score of 10–2 in consecutive games, to lift them well clear of trouble. Their inconsistent form would continue to dog them throughout the campaign, however, and City finally finished in 11th position. The West Ham game would remain one of only a few really positive memories of that season and would typify the worth of Bell to the Blues, even when not fully fit.

18 Top Dogs

City 3, Sunderland 2
Date: 11 May 1991
Competition: Division One
City: Margetson, Hill, Pointon, Heath, Hendry, Redmond,
White, Brennan, Quinn, Harper, Clarke (Beckford)
Attendance: 39,194

Where was the author? On the Kippax, about midway up and across.

Finishing the season with a game affecting the relegation places and having Luton Town involved in the dogfight are ingredients to make even the most hardened City supporter turn towards the drinks cabinet. David Pleat and Raddy Antic still hold an unwelcome but steadfast place in City folklore, even after all these years.

However, on Saturday 11 May 1991, a funny thing happened. City entered the last weekend of the season with no relegation worries and found themselves intertwined in a plot that offered them an unusually nerveless cameo role. It was Sunderland who arrived firmly under the relegation spotlight on this occasion with the Blues poised to wrap up a magnificent season under Peter Reid and Sam Ellis – the best in the league since 1978, in fact.

The achievement was all the more impressive taking into account that Reid had only taken on this his first job at managerial level after Howard Kendall had jumped ship to Goodison Park the previous December. The Wearsiders arrived at Maine Road needing a win to take them above Luton – so long as the Hatters slipped up at home to Derby County, who City had relegated two weeks before in the famous 'Niall Quinn Game', where he scored a goal and then replaced Tony Coton in goal and saved a penalty from Dean Saunders.

This was the kind of afternoon made for City. Maine Road was heaving with the attendance just a fraction under 40,000 and a huge 8,000-strong contingent from Sunderland added to the carnival atmosphere inside the ground. In a pulsating first half, both sides netted twice. Quinn, ending a fantastic campaign during which he'd led the line with grace and goals, put City ahead after only 10 minutes. Defender John Kay got in a mess from a long ball into Sunderland's box and the tall striker coolly slotted home. It was almost half time before Sunderland recovered, but they did so in style, Marco Gabbiadini heading in at the end of a sweeping move up the left, again involving Kay and then City old boy Gary Bennett headed home after a huge scramble in the City box to make it 2–1 minutes later.

David White's late winner against Sunderland ensured the Blues finished above Manchester United for the first time in thirteen years.

With the Sunderland hordes hanging onto the fencing at the front of the Platt Lane stand, the atmosphere was electric. The reporter at Luton then told those listening to their radios, 'If I tell you that Mick Harford has scored here . . .' The crowd rose again, only to find that the Derby forward had scored in his own net to put Luton one up! It was cruel to say the least. As the atmosphere among the away fans shifted, Quinn burst onto a loose ball in the Sunderland area (this time the nervous Gary Owers kicking air instead of leather) and hammered a low shot past Norman to even the scores once more and send the teams in level at the break.

It seemed that the old ground would pop, such was the pandemonium. City had their own agenda to follow with the chance of ending the season ahead of Manchester United, so there were no thoughts of sympathy towards their struggling opponents. In the space of five minutes Sunderland had equalised, gone ahead, seen Luton score and then conceded one themselves. It was hard on Sunderland, but typical of the never-say-die attitude that the City of Peter Reid's stewardship possessed. Reid had started the game with Quinn, David White and Wayne Clarke up front, in an attempt to have the same effect as the fortnight before when City had knocked in five at Villa Park.

Increasingly desperate, Sunderland were unable to find a way through in the second period as they threw numbers forward at every opportunity. Both Gabbiadini and Davenport found their paths blocked by heroic keeping from City stand-in Martyn Margetson and, as time ticked by, it seemed obvious that their top-flight status was all but over.

One final surge forward by City brought the reward their football deserved. As the ball arrived at the feet of Adrian Heath wide on the right, he chipped a cross up to the far post where the incoming David White tucked it away with his head, colliding with the post in the process, to send Maine Road into a frenzy. The home supporters knew the magnitude of the goal meant that, after thirteen years of finishing below United in the table, White's goal took City to fifth in the table, one place above United for the first time in more than a decade.

19   Home at Last

City 2, Sheffield United 1
Date: 25 August 1923
Competition: Division One
City: Mitchell, Cookson, Fletcher, Hamill, Woosnam, Pringle, Donaldson, Roberts, Johnson, Barnes, Murphy
Attendance: 56,993

Where was the author? Not born yet! And I suspect neither were you . . .

It was a proud day for Manchester City and their fans when the Blues walked out into their brand new Moss Side home for the first time in August 1923. The crowd of 56,993 was a new attendance record for the club who had left the far less grand surroundings of Hyde Road a few months earlier.

Their old home and its unique atmosphere had not been completely forgotten, though. Goal posts and several turnstiles were integrated at Maine Road while the old main stand roof was transported to Halifax Town's Shay stadium to keep the rain off an entirely new set of shivering souls. The total cost of the new stadium is almost impossible to trace, but various reports seem to suggest it was in the region of £150,000. Designed by Manchester architect Charles Swain and built by Sir Robert McAlpine in less than twelve months, the whole ambitious project was a tribute to all concerned in both its design and construction.

Maine Road's capacity was more than double that of Hyde Road and was built to house approximately 80,000. In England only Wembley Stadium, opened just months earlier, could hold more fans. The vast bank of terracing facing the players as they ran out was known originally as the 'popular side' (later to become the Kippax) and was where the main bulk of City fans gathered for the opening match – a trend that would continue until the ground's closure eighty years later.

With only the main stand roofed, much of the noise generated by the crowd was lost to the open air above their heads but there was still a tremendous atmosphere as Ernest Magnall's side took to the field of play. Legendary all-round sportsman Max Woosnam was named as captain and it was he who led the Blues out as the assembled band played 'Ours is a nice house, ours is'.

Woosnam had missed the whole of the 1922/3 campaign with a fractured leg sustained by colliding with a wooden fence at Hyde Road, and also missed the chance to defend his Wimbledon doubles title during his absence! No doubt immensely proud, the captain rallied the side to ensure the first game at Maine Road began with a victory. The Lord Mayor of Manchester was then introduced to the players before ceremoniously kicking the match off before Tommy Johnson did it for real moments later on referee Howcroft's whistle, beginning a whole new era for the Blues.

Sammy Cookson and Eli Fletcher, like Woosnam, had returned after lengthy lay-offs and Alec Donaldson, a recent signing from Bolton Wanderers, made his full league debut. Sheffield United were more than capable of ruining the day and had taken three out of the four points available in the previous season's corresponding fixtures.

A tight first half ended without either side testing the new netting, despite Tommy Johnson and Horace Barnes forcing the visiting 'keeper Gough into a couple of decent saves. City came out for the second half determined to see off the Blades' challenge and the prestigious honour of the first ever goal scored at Maine Road went to the prolific Barnes on 68 minutes after connecting with debutant Donaldson's cross. Strike partner Johnson made it 2–0 just three minutes later and the Blues could have really begun life with a Manchester 14 postcode in style when they were awarded a penalty and a chance to go 3–0 up shortly after.

But, just as Barnes forever etched his name into the record books by scoring the first goal, Frank Roberts followed suit by becoming the first player to miss a penalty at the new ground. Despite the new introduction of the arc on the edge of the box which allowed the taker a good run up to the spot, he hit his shot straight at Gough to give the visitors an unlikely lifeline.

The Blades, reduced to ten men through injury, duly scored in the 88th minute through Harry Johnson to ensure a tense finish – one of hundreds to follow – but City held out for the victory the huge crowd had demanded. For skipper Woosnam it was to be his only league appearance of the season – no doubt his desire to lead out his team for such an historic occasion had clouded his judgement regarding the extent of his injury or rather he was determined to play at any cost. His decision had not adversely affected the day's play and Maine Road was up and running with the best start possible.

20　Rebirth of the Blues

CITY 2, STOKE CITY 1
DATE: 29 DECEMBER 1998
COMPETITION: DIVISION TWO
CITY: WEAVER, CROOKS, EDGHILL, WIEKENS, VAUGHAN, HORLOCK,
BROWN, POLLOCK, TAYLOR, BISHOP (GOATER 46 MINS), DICKOV
ATTENDANCE: 30,478

Where was the author? In the seated Kippax, lower tier with Santy and Donna.

For any game in 1998 to qualify as a classic match, the circumstances had to be special. With City at the lowest ebb in their history, wallowing in mid-table in their first ever season outside the top two divisions, something above the ordinary was required to kick-start a late bid for promotion. The Christmas period had borne witness to a slight stirring with a soggy, rain-swept 1–0 victory at Wrexham. That this had followed an embarrassing 2–1 defeat at York City and several other poor performances still did not bode well. City were showing only occasional signs of acclimatising to their harsh, unwanted new surroundings.

The arrival of long-time leaders Stoke City to Maine Road for the last game of the year on 28 December, therefore, gave the Blues the chance to show that the previous win at Wrexham, hard-earned and unpleasant on the eye as it had been, was not just another flash in the pan but the start of something more solid to build on. As manager Joe Royle would often reiterate, the size of City's following during this season of purgatory was quite overwhelming for all concerned. This could work in two ways, Royle maintained, either as a dead weight around the neck or as a galvanising force.

'There is a certain element who are becoming very vociferous and very negative,' wrote Royle in his pre-match programme notes for Stoke. Continuing with the same theme, he said, 'I can understand why two chairmen and a succession of managers have been hounded out of this place.' Perhaps shocked by the harshness of Royle's words, the crowd's reaction was exemplary. For the first time since the opening day victory over Blackpool, the evidence was there for all to see that the home crowd's influence on the legs and minds of the City players could work greatly to the team's benefit.

Stoke had led the division all season but, entering this match in third place, were waning under the pressure of a lengthy period out ahead of the pack. With more than 30,000 jammed inside Maine Road, it was

Paul Dickov played an integral part in City's 2–1 win over Stoke in 1998 – the start of a surge towards the Division Two play-offs.

the home side which had the better of the opening passage of play and, although City had a goal disallowed when Taylor's 10th-minute header was ruled out by a fussy linesman, Stoke gradually took command and took the lead with a well-worked goal after 30 minutes. City's defence appeared to stand and watch as Sigurdsson rose to head in after a simple move had carved the Blues open down their right flank.

Royle made a vital change at half time, bringing on Goater to accompany Dickov and Taylor up front and taking off the unlucky Ian Bishop. Once again City tore into the visitors and this time their energetic play reaped immediate dividends. A mistake at the back produced a scuffle between Goater and the pressurised 'keeper Carl Muggleton, allowing the ball to be rolled across the area for Dickov to tap in. Maine Road erupted and, with the forceful and noisy backing of the crowd, City grew in stature and confidence.

Stoke were pinned back for long periods, but managed to hold on until five minutes from time when Dickov's speculative cross from far out on the left was headed in majestically by Gareth Taylor – his first goal in City colours since a £400,000 transfer from Sheffield United eight weeks earlier. With Maine Road in a tumult of noise, the visitors could not muster an answer to this late surge and City captured what was at the time a prize scalp.

The manager's concerns about the fans had been answered in no uncertain terms. The wall of noise created in the second half had persuaded the players to give everything. 'The crowd will remember the second half for the guts and passion we showed and football we played at times. In the end, justice was done,' said the City boss afterwards.

As the crowd trickled out of the old stadium, a palpable sense of belief was in the air. Everyone had done their bit. The feeling was very much that this could be the catalyst to set the Blues on a run towards glorious promotion in May – all of which was proved correct, although the manner that it would finally be achieved could not have been imagined on that biting December evening.

21   Trans-Europe Express

CITY 1, BORUSSIA MÖNCHENGLADBACH 1
DATE: 7 MARCH 1979
COMPETITION: UEFA CUP, 4TH ROUND
CITY: CORRIGAN, DONACHIE, POWER, REID, WATSON, BOOTH,
CHANNON, VILJOEN, KIDD, HARTFORD, BARNES
ATTENDANCE: 39,005

*Where was the author? In the Main Stand for this one, on the front row
by the manager's dug-out.*

'Kevin Keegan, the English jewel in the crown of West German
football is backing Manchester City to topple Borussia
Mönchengladbach in the UEFA Cup quarter-final,' announced
the *Daily Express* on Friday 19 January, the day of the draw for the last
eight for what was then the third of UEFA's yearly tournaments. This was
January 1979 and City's opponents were one of the strongest teams in
(then West) Germany.

Having already dealt admirably with Twente Enschede, Standard Liege
and AC Milan, hopes were high that City could salvage some glory from
a season that had flopped badly. Malcolm Allison's 'Second Coming' had
proved to be a disaster and the Blues, tipped at the start of the campaign
to be in the final shake-up for the title, were well adrift in lower mid-table.
The Germans were not without their problems either, slowly decreasing
in power from the mighty outfit which had dominated the Bundesliga
and jousted with Liverpool in UEFA and European Cup finals in the
early 1970s (many still remembered with awe Keegan's last match in a
Liverpool shirt as he gave the limpet marking of German stopper Bertie
Vogts the run-around in Rome as Liverpool took the European crown in
1977).

Typical of Allison's approach in this period, faced with the dilemma
of who was to replace the suspended Gary Owen (Owen had kung-fu
kicked his way into a red card in Liege in the second round in the
previous November), the maverick Allison opted to give Nicky Reid a
debut at the age of eighteen and ask him to mark the then Footballer of
the Year Alan Simonsen. This with Colin Bell and Kaziu Deyna, European
veterans both, ready to come in for Owen and shore up the middle of the
park. Allison was a gambler, however, and Reid was chosen.

Reid played well enough in the first leg, considering the almighty
burden bestowed upon him (Allison would launch 16-year-old Tommy
Caton with similar staggering confidence at the start of the next season),

Kaziu Deyna shows Malcolm Allison what he's missed with a stunning volley away to Borussia Mönchengladbach in 1979.

but City struggled to get through a rugged German rearguard, backed by some great goalkeeping from the giant Wolfgang Kneib. Unable to build on the 25th-minute lead given to them by Channon, the Blues were pegged back mid-way through the second period when Simonsen's trickery on the wing opened up a chance for Ewald Lienen to equalise crisply.

The Germans tested Corrigan towards the end and Bruns' shot smacked off a post and resulted in City losing their shape. Even the normally mild-mannered Paul Power started a multi-player punch-up after a robust challenge on the Mönchengladbach 'keeper. Borussia were not entirely alone being pleased with the 1–1 draw. Allison, though, later commented 'I would not say they were defensive, let's just say they got all eleven players behind the ball every time we came within 40 yards of their goal!'

The second leg, played in front of a Bokelberg Stadium packed to its 35,000 capacity saw a gutsy City performance undone by sheer bad luck just before the interval. With the game ebbing and flowing and little to choose between the sides, Tony Henry sent a screaming shot onto the Borussia post in the 44th minute. Picking up the loose ball, the Germans swept straight upfield and Kulik buried a shot to send his side in at the interval 1–0 up. Allison would later say that 'the goal just before half time broke our neck,' but in truth City were to take quite a hammering in the second half, with the Danes Simonsen and Kalle Del'Haye attacking down either flank in mesmerising fashion. By the 72nd minute City were three down to goals from Bruns and the menacing Del'Haye and heading for the exit.

It had been a titanic struggle but the Germans on this form held just too many aces for the Blues to deal with. Deyna's belated introduction for the struggling Nicky Reid, however, sparked a revival and his sweetly struck volley from Channon's pass brought City back into the game, if not really the tie. City had been steamrollered in the second half by the all-out attacking wing-play of Udo Lattek's Borussia, who would go on to win the competition against Eintracht Frankfurt in the final.

It had been a fantastic journey through to the quarter-finals, illuminating what might have been in an increasingly disappointing season. No one present at either match against Borussia Mönchengladbach could possibly have realised at the time how many years of torment were to follow before the Blues once again graced the playing fields of continental Europe.

22   Return of the Law Man

CITY 3, BIRMINGHAM CITY 1
DATE: 25 AUGUST 1974
COMPETITION: DIVISION ONE
CITY: CORRIGAN, BOOK (CARRADOUS), DONACHIE, DOYLE, BOOTH,
OAKES, SUMMERBEE, BELL, LEE, LAW, MARSH
ATTENDANCE: 34,178

Where was the author? On holiday with my dad in the Lakes.

'It will be really great going back to my old club. But I can tell you that if City hadn't made a bid for me, I would have packed in the game.' So spoke Denis Law on the eve of the 1973/4 season, his last in English football, as he prepared to make his second debut in the sky blue of City. He had signed for a single season, with an option for a second, after surprisingly being given a free from Old Trafford.

New City manager Johnny Hart admitted taking a gamble on the man he wanted to join Colin Bell, Francis Lee, Mike Summerbee and the unsettled Rodney Marsh to make an irresistible front line. 'Both Denis and myself stand to be shot at,' added Hart, alluding to the throw of the dice he was taking. Immediately Marsh was removed from the transfer list and Law scored his first goal for the first team in a pre-season game against Oldham.

City launched the season with a home defeat against Burnley in the Charity Shield, but, as the sun came out over an expectant Maine Road a week later, the scene was set for a memorable performance and a vintage display from Law. More than 34,000 made their way to the old ground to witness Law's second coming and they were soon singing his praises as he put the Blues ahead against Birmingham, swinging his right foot at a headed pass from Bell at the North Stand end following great work from Marsh and Lee down the left flank.

By half time Birmingham were level after Trevor Francis, later to do much the same for City in one injury-plagued season, ran at the hosts' rearguard down the right flank and, beating them with a combination of pace and trickery, crossed low for Bob Hatton to deflect into the net.

In the second half City quickly regained the initiative. First, from Summerbee's corner, the Birmingham defence failed to get a proper connection with the ball as it fell to Bell on the edge of the box. He controlled it on his chest, went past the lunge of a defender and despatched it calmly past Dave Latchford for 2–1.

Then came the moment of the match. With Birmingham beginning to tire in the sun and City beginning to showboat somewhat, the ball fell to Marsh on the Kippax side of Birmingham's penalty area. He brought the ball under control and waited for the defender, Roger Hynd, to face him properly, before wafting his foot over the ball, as if he didn't quite know what he was going to do with it. Suitably off-balance, Hynd fell to one side as Marsh dummied again and went the other way, crossing to the far post with his left foot, where Law climbed to head home his second of the game.

'The perfect finish to Denis Law's perfect day,' chirruped a young John Motson on that night's *Match of the Day* and few could argue. Law's double set City off to a great start to the season, which would ultimately end trophy-less, despite a heroic run to the League Cup Final, where Wolves' understudy 'keeper Gary Pearce would play a blinder to keep out Law, Marsh and the rest of the five-man City attack in a heart-breaking performance.

Law's legs would eventually fail him, but not before he had summoned the strength for one last flick off his boot to back-heel the ball into the net at Old Trafford one more time, effectively confirming United's relegation. The goal would be his last in league football before the season came to a fitting end playing in the dark blue of Scotland in the 1974 World Cup finals in West Germany, where the Scots remained unbeaten, but went out after games against Zaire, Brazil and Yugoslavia.

23   For Whom the Bell Tolls

CITY 3, FC TWENTE 2
DATE: 27 SEPTEMBER 1978
COMPETITION: UEFA CUP, 1ST ROUND, 2ND LEG
CITY: CORRIGAN, CLEMENTS, POWER, VILJOEN (BELL), WATSON,
P. FUTCHER, CHANNON, OWEN, KIDD, HARTFORD, BARNES
ATTENDANCE: 29,330

Where was the author? At home on a school night, wishing I was there.

The following quote from John Roberts in his report in the *Guardian* on Thursday 28 September 1978 may sound vaguely familiar, 'Manchester City took their supporters on the accustomed roller-coaster ride before defeating their admirably resilient counterparts . . .'

How often has this term been used in describing the club's history, its fortunes and even, as in this case, individual City matches? The Blues seem to have spent most of their history defining the phrase in its finest detail since the year dot and the City fans have the creases across their brows to prove it.

Having failed at the first hurdle of their previous three UEFA Cup campaigns, Tony Book's side were especially keen to make it through to the second round and hopefully draw one of Europe's big guns. A gritty 1–1 draw in Holland against FC Twente of Enschede two weeks earlier now made everything possible for the second leg at Maine Road with Dave Watson's flying header in the first leg setting the Blues up nicely.

Watson was heard to say after the first leg, 'We have seen the best of Twente tonight, but they haven't seen the best of us yet!' At least one half of the defender's statement would seem wishful thinking when the second leg finally got under way two weeks later.

City started well enough with Peter Barnes and Gary Owen creating a couple of presentable chances for Brian Kidd. Perhaps rusty from missing the six previous games with a broken toe, City's curly-haired no. 9 failed to put either opportunity away, though it seemed to matter little after Owen's shimmy and cross proved impossible to defend and Dutch World Cup man Piet Wildschut turned the ball into his own net.

The impression that City were striding confidently towards the next round continued for most of the first half with Kidd finally finding the back of the net, only to have his effort disallowed and Owen seeing a shot strike the post.

However, the Dutch side were right back in the tie within minutes of the restart after Overweg's daisy cutter of a free kick skidded past the haphazardly arranged wall and proceeded to zip past Joe Corrigan, with the surprised 'keeper realising too late that his defensive barrier had crumbled.

With Twente's tails up and the sniff of a winning goal in the offing, the match began to ebb and flow at breakneck speed. Book, introducing Colin Bell for Colin Viljoen, attempted to reintroduce some urgency to City's midfield prompting, as Twente were winning more and more possession in the middle of the park.

It was Bell's first appearance of the season after his comeback from terrible injury the previous Boxing Day. Sure enough, his first touch was the prelude to four consecutive corners as the Blues upped the ante. Bell then put Kenny Clements through with a deft pass and nearly caught the Dutch 'keeper with a clever lob. The crowd was purring to see the old master performing so effortlessly.

Shortly after, City were ahead again – Kidd, received the ball, performed a pirouette to shake his marker, stepped forward a little and buried a vicious shot from 30 yards. To Twente's credit, they wasted no time in applying more pressure of their own and Corrigan was forced to tip a shot onto the post before the game swept to the other end. Channon's header was parried out to Bell who smacked the ball home on the volley.

With four minutes to go, Gritter, living up to his name, hauled the plucky Eredivisie side back into the game by making it 3–2 as City refused to take the easy option of closing up shop. The Dutch produced a barnstorming finish, but couldn't break City down a third time as the European jinx was finally laid to rest.

24   St Francis of Man City

STOKE CITY 1, CITY 3
DATE: 5 SEPTEMBER 1981
COMPETITION: DIVISION ONE
CITY: CORRIGAN, RANSON, MCDONALD, REID, CATON, POWER,
O'NEILL, GOW, HARTFORD, FRANCIS, REEVES SUB: BOYER
ATTENDANCE: 25,256

---

*Where was the author? Listening to Brian Clarke again – we didn't really
have that much spare money for away trips . . .*

When Trevor Francis walked onto the sun-lit Victoria Ground
pitch at Stoke at 2.55 p.m. on 5 September 1981, he
carried the high hopes of the blue half of Manchester on
his not-too-broad shoulders. When he walked off it at the end of a
tumultuous match, he said, 'I'll never forget my one million pound
debut for Nottingham Forest at Ipswich. After thirty minutes the fans
were singing "what a waste of money!" I didn't give them the same
opportunity this time!'

After a long struggle to find a decent striker, John Bond had finally
managed to beat Ron Atkinson to the coveted Forest striker's signature
and make him the first player ever to cost £1m twice. United had wanted
to trade former Forest striker Gary Birtles for Francis, but that idea had
been kiboshed by Brian Clough, owing to the fact that Birtles' flow of
goals at Old Trafford had never breached the level of a parched trickle.

City had started the season well enough with a 2–1 home win over
West Brom, but it had been the midweek draw at lowly Notts County
which concerned Bond who believed the Blues had not got enough
firepower up-front to take the team on from the previous May's FA Cup
final defeat to Spurs. Francis was spotted in the stands at Meadow Lane
that night and Bond raised the stakes in the after-match press conference
by saying, 'After tonight's game, I'm moving in even stronger for Trevor.'
Assistant John Benson added, 'If we had had Trevor in the side tonight,
we would have won it by half time.'

The travelling City army numbered more than 10,000 at the Victoria
Ground after something akin to Francis hysteria broke out. They were
in good spirits but even the most optimistic among them couldn't have
guessed that Francis was about to explode into their consciousness
with a debut that would only be matched sporadically thereafter. With
Peter Fox performing heroics from the beginning, Stoke, starting the
game as surprise early leaders of the division, were under intense

City manager John Bond masterminded the signing of Trevor Francis in 1981.

pressure. They held out until the 35th minute when Bobby McDonald's long clearance found new boy Francis running free in a promising position. He proceeded to turn the gangly Brendan O'Callaghan inside out before moving inside Ray Evans and again meeting O'Callaghan tracking back as best he could. Rounding the defender for a second time, he hit a low shot through Fox's legs to the delight of the Blues fans behind the goal.

Stoke battled back after the break and Chapman equalised after an hour, running towards Corrigan with Tommy Caton in hot pursuit and sliding the ball past City's giant goalkeeper. City moved Phil Boyer into the injured Paul Power's midfield slot and the battle raged again. Within five minutes, the Blues had regained the lead, as Gerry Gow put Francis away down the right. His centre got stuck in a group of bodies and Kevin Reeves eventually prodded home with ex-City stalwart Mike Doyle helpless to intervene.

By the time Francis had wrapped the game up with his second and City's third, the fans were comparing his debut favourably with those of Denis Law, Colin Bell and Dennis Tueart before him. Francis had only had lunchtime to acclimatise to his new surroundings (John Bond had famously brought the new signing into the hotel where City's players were having lunch and said, somewhat unnecessarily, 'This is Trevor, he's here to give us the confidence to win things').

Afterwards the press pack was eating out of the striker's hand. Although his magic would rub off on the rest of the team, Francis would only play one injury-ravaged season for City before being sold to Italian Serie A outfit Sampdoria to lessen the terrible financial burden being carried by the club at the time. He would later be quoted on the subject of Peter Swales' profligacy that the former City chairman was a man who went out to buy a Jaguar and came back with a Rolls. Trevor's self-image was never low, that can be confidently said!

Bond's dream of domination would turn to ashes the following season when he resigned after a shambolic cup defeat at Brighton. With Francis' unforgettable debut fading to the back of Blues fans' minds, City went down to the Second Division just a year and a half after his sunshine debut in the Potteries.

25 Boro Downed

City 4, Middlesbrough 0
Date: 21 January 1976
Competition: League Cup Semi-Final, 2nd Leg
City: Corrigan, Barrett, Donachie, Doyle, Clements, Oakes,
Power, Keegan, Royle, Hartford, Barnes
Attendance: 44,426

Where was the author? Not sure for this one, but not at the match.

During the 1970s, City were the team to beat for anyone aspiring to win the League Cup. Finalists three times in that decade, City carried off the trophy twice, beating West Brom and Newcastle, the latter in 1976 being the very well-documented last bit of silver the Blues got their hands on. To get to that final in '76, City had struggled past an odd variety of sides, from Norwich and Nottingham Forest in the early rounds to the sound thrashing of Manchester United in the fourth – the game when Colin Bell suffered his horrific knee injury – and a 4–2 win over Fourth-Division Mansfield Town in the quarter-finals.

This set up a semi-final over two legs with Jackie Charlton's Middlesbrough, a team hewn out of the same stubborn, no-nonsense granite as their bull-necked manager who had been the rock of Leeds United's defence during his distinguished playing career. Boro won the first leg 1–0 in a tight and passionate game at Ayresome Park, setting up the Maine Road second leg beautifully. The stage was set for a memorable night and the Blues would not disappoint.

City boss Tony Book kept faith with the side that had beaten West Ham 3–0 the previous Saturday, which meant there was no recall for the fit-again defensive lynchpin Tommy Booth. The much-needed confidence-booster over the Hammers ended a run of four successive 1–0 defeats and restored the players' faith at a point where things could have turned decidedly pear-shaped.

Boro had come out of the Second Division on the back of a stern defence that gave little away, so most pundits felt that City were up against it to make it to their third League Cup Final in six years. What followed on the night of the second leg was a City performance that had the old ground in raptures. With injury and suspension robbing City of three England internationals, the Blues not only made up the deficit, they pulverised their north-eastern opponents with a four-goal salvo.

It was a trio of youngsters who took the plaudits on the night: Paul Power, who had played his first full game in the first leg, Ged Keegan, playing only his sixth full game for the seniors and Peter Barnes, at nineteen, about to embark on a glittering international career. Barnes, incidentally, had broken his nose against West Ham four days earlier, but it wouldn't affect him in the slightest for this match. The tie swung City's way right from the start. The early breakthrough, so vital in such finely balanced ties, came as Barnes chased a seemingly over-hit cross by Asa Hartford with the visitors' defence anticipating it would go out of play. However, the young winger sprinted in on the blind side and hit an instant left-foot cross on the run back into the box where Keegan headed thunderously past Jim Platt.

City nudged ahead on aggregate after only eleven minutes of a breathless start. Colin Barrett's cross appeared to touch Keegan's hand as it slid across the edge of the box, but the referee waved play-on and Alan Oakes hit a screaming left-foot drive into the Middlesbrough net.

The inexperience of Paul Power almost let the Teessiders back into the game on 17 minutes when David Armstrong seized on a weak back-pass, rounded Corrigan and slapped his shot onto the post. With the tie on a knife-edge, that coat of paint effectively sealed the fate of Big Jack's men. This was to be City's night, and, as Craggs lost a square ball from Murdoch in no man's land, Barnes stormed through the middle to sweep the doubts away with the third of the evening, planting a low shot past the advancing Platt. The final goal, a minute from time, was a neat replica of the third, as the hapless Craggs again was to blame when he sent a poor pass into the path of Joe Royle who strode forward to belt his shot past Platt and so continue his record of scoring in every round.

There were eleven heroes in blue shirts that night with all the youngsters impressive throughout, but Royle, Oakes, Asa Hartford, Kenny Clements and Joe Corrigan were all in the frame for man-of-the-match honours. Big Joe left the pitch in tears. 'The emotion was just too much for me,' explained City's giant 'keeper. Skipper Mike Doyle drove his side on relentlessly from the back in what many considered was his greatest-ever defensive display.

Tony Book, who had led City to all their earlier triumphs, was especially proud to be given the chance to repeat those efforts as manager and joked, 'Wait until we get our first team out!' He added, 'If I had to pick out one man, I would nominate Gerard Keegan. When kids come into the team and play like that, it gives you a feeling you can't explain.'

Jack Charlton was not in the best of moods after the game and claimed that City had scored four goals with their only four shots of the evening, but then, Big Jack had the ability to turn a pint of milk sour with an unsavoury glance if he so wished.

Ged Keegan would hold onto his place for the final against Newcastle and Barnes would once again reveal his rich promise with the opening goal on an afternoon still fêted to this day by Blues supporters for Dennis Tueart's Wembley gymnastics – and rightly so.

Peter Barnes – when he was good, he was very, very good, as Middlesbrough found to their cost in the League Cup semi-final second leg in 1976.

26   A Rare Victory Indeed

CITY 2, LIVERPOOL 1
DATE: 21 AUGUST 1991
COMPETITION: DIVISION ONE
CITY: COTON, HILL, POINTON, REID (HEATH), CURLE, REDMOND,
WHITE, BRIGHTWELL, QUINN, MEGSON, BRENNAN
ATTENDANCE: 37,322

Where was the author? Relocated in the Kippax, centre right.

Under the guidance of Peter Reid, City started the 1991/2 season with a hard-fought 1–0 win at Coventry, thanks to Niall Quinn's headed goal, and they went into the first home game of the season against Liverpool determined to harry the Merseysiders out of their cultured rhythm. It was a feature of Reid's City sides that they were seldom found wanting when they had a battle on their hands.

So it was on this August evening as over 37,000 took the opportunity to welcome the Blues into the new season. While the visitors had added the likes of Mark Wright and Dean Saunders to an already sumptuous squad, Reid's main summer signing had been Keith Curle from Wimbledon for £2.5m. He would play his part in a great all-round performance in what was a tremendous game from start to finish. City tore into Liverpool from the first minute, never allowing ball-players such as John Barnes and a young Steve McManaman time to settle into their stride. With Wright struggling to contain the flailing limbs of Niall Quinn and Ian Brightwell's energetic midfield exertions snuffing out the usually dominant Steve McMahon, City had the foundations to go on and beat Liverpool for the first time since Boxing Day 1985 and it was Quinn who provided the opening from which City took the lead. With half an hour played, he lobbed a glorious pass over the top of David Burrows into the path of David White, whose pace had already taken him clear of the remainder of the Liverpool defence and a typical slide rule finish past Bruce Grobbelaar put the Blues 1–0 up. It wasn't until midway through the second half that the same combination put City firmly in the driving seat. Quinn's flick-on sent White hurtling towards the Liverpool box with Wright once again trailing in his wake. As White looked up, he unleashed an unstoppable drive, which rocketed past Grobbelaar and hit the underside of the bar before bouncing away to safety. It seemed to take an age for referee Paul Vanes to make his mind up, but after clarifying with his linesman, he pointed to the centre circle and the packed Kippax went wild as a result while White was mobbed by his team-mates. Those sitting comfortably in the Main Stand that night were treated to one of the last views of the giant old terrace vibrating to a capacity crowd really letting its hair down, the scene an immense mass of writhing humanity.

There was still time for the inevitable Liverpool comeback, led by McManaman. His diving header reduced the deficit and then, as City seemed to be home and dry, Andy Hill's outstretched leg brought down £2.9m Saunders. The Welshman dusted himself down and perhaps mindful of Niall Quinn's penalty save against him the previous season when Derby were relegated at Maine Road, Saunders walloped his penalty against the underside of the bar before it was cleared to safety. Again the home fans went crazy and moments later they were celebrating an encouraging 2–1 win. A 3–2 win over Crystal Palace a few days later would put them top of the table with a 100 per cent record. White, meanwhile would hit another double against Liverpool in the return match at Anfield, confirming an end to the era where Liverpool only had to show up to guarantee victory over the Blues.

David White –scored four goals against Liverpool in 1991/2.

27   Young at Heart

CITY 1, LEICESTER CITY 0
DATE: 26 APRIL 1969
COMPETITION: FA CUP FINAL
CITY: DOWD, BOOK, PARDOE, DOYLE, BOOTH, OAKES, SUMMERBEE,
BELL, LEE, COLEMAN, YOUNG
ATTENDANCE: 100,000

Where was the author? Still too small to know football existed.

City were back at Wembley for the first time in thirteen years. Having already surrendered the league title crown they'd won twelve months earlier thanks to a disappointing campaign, the FA Cup represented a very acceptable consolation prize.

Leicester City were the opposition in the final tie and the teams had already met twice in the league that season, with the Foxes beating the defending champions 3–0 at Filbert Street and City winning the return game 2–0 courtesy of a Mike Summerbee brace.

The Blues had been struggling in mid-table, but had begun to show flashes of the genius that had enchanted the nation as Christmas approached by beating West Brom 5–1, Burnley 7–0 and Coventry City 4–2. It was too little, too late, however and the team instead seemed to turn their attention to the last piece of silverware they could still win – the FA Cup.

They began their quest with an unconvincing 1–0 win over Luton Town at Maine Road courtesy of a Francis Lee goal in front of 37,120 fans. The draw for the next round was not so kind with a difficult looking trip to St James' Park – scene of the championship clinching 4–3 win the previous May, but a venue where they had already lost 1–0 to Newcastle in the league fixture a couple of months earlier.

With more than 55,000 packed in and the Gallowgate End in full voice, Joe Mercer and Malcolm Allison knew that this was a game that a gung-ho attitude would likely end in defeat. The return of skipper Tony Book, who had missed the first half of the campaign with an Achilles injury, could not have been timed any better and City proved resilient and difficult to break down. They left the North-East with a 0–0 draw and finished the job off four days later with a 2–0 win in front of a massive crowd of 60,844.

The fifth round saw City paired with Second-Division Blackburn Rovers at Ewood Park. The freezing February weather put paid to several league fixtures and this was the club's first game for a month, but there were no signs of rust as two goals each from Tony Coleman and Lee put the Blues into the quarter-finals following a resounding 4–1 win.

Now only Tottenham stood between the Blues and a place in the semi-finals and in front of nearly 50,000 Maine Road fans, Lee grabbed the only goal of a tightly-contested match – the ballet on ice was now a distant memory. March was proving an enjoyable month for the Blue half of Manchester with Summerbee securing a 1–0 win over United at Old Trafford in the derby, while the draw for the semis pitted the Blues with Everton, though the Toffees' two previous league meetings suggested the Toffees would start as strong favourites.

The tie was played at Villa Park in front of 63,025 and proved a tactical battle with both teams cancelling each other out for long periods. Then, with seconds remaining, Tommy Booth popped up to score his second goal of the season – a dramatic winner to send the Blues to Wembley and around 30,000 City fans into raptures.

A backlog of fixtures meant five league games in fifteen days and hardly surprisingly, a tired City team lost three of the matches, including a clash with leaders Leeds United a day after a 2–0 home win over Leicester City.

Cup fever had gripped Manchester and all the tickets were sold soon after going on sale but the club's form going into the final was poor and successive defeats at West Brom and Southampton – without a goal in either game – hardly inspired confidence among the supporters.

After City had used a touch of Allison psychology by deliberately keeping Leicester waiting in the tunnel for a minute, they lined up alongside their opponents and walked out to the deafening cheers of 100,000 fans. It was a proud moment for both Joe Mercer and Leicester City boss Frank O'Farrell as they led their teams out for this showpiece occasion. For Leicester in particular, reaching the final had been a triumph over adversity after having the shock result of the competition by beating Liverpool 1–0 at Anfield – even more impressive considering they'd lost 16 games away from home in the league and would be relegated just two weeks later!

The Blues turned on the style, attacking from the start but Leicester, revelling in their role as underdogs, created chances as the match ebbed and flowed. The Foxes were playing their third Wembley final of the decade and were determined not to make it a third defeat in succession and both Clarke and Rodrigues could have given them the lead – Clarke seeing his shot brilliantly saved by Harry Dowd and Rodrigues somehow missing a cross from a couple of yards out as he sliced the ball wide. Just three minutes after that miss, City struck. Summerbee wriggled past lunging challenges from Nish and Woollett, before pulling the ball back for Neil Young to slam the ball past Peter Shilton and into the roof of the net to give his team a 1–0 lead.

Dowd preserved City's slender advantage with several fine saves after the break and was the Blues' outstanding performer on the day – the fact that he was man-of-the-match proves Leicester were more than a tad unfortunate on the day, but despite their best efforts, City hung on to claim a memorable win.

As HRH Princess Anne handed the FA Cup over to skipper Tony Book, the former Bath City full-back must have been pinching himself. 'Skip' had been playing Southern League football for Bath City just five years earlier and now he was again holding aloft the most famous cup in the world as captain of the Blues – could life get any better?

Tony Book holds aloft the FA Cup after a 1–0 win over Leicester City.

28   Highbury High

ARSENAL 2, CITY 3
DATE: 4 OCTOBER 1975
COMPETITION: DIVISION ONE
CITY: CORRIGAN, CLEMENTS, DONACHIE, DOYLE, OAKES, BELL,
WATSON, MARSH (POWER), TUEART, ROYLE, HARTFORD
ATTENDANCE: 24,928

Where was the author? Most likely at Cubs!

Preparing to visit Highbury in October 1975 was not quite the daunting task it is today. Arsenal's fortunes had withered after their great double-winning era and the team was slowing down considerably by the mid-1970s. Youthful replacements such as Liam Brady, Frank Stapleton and David O'Leary were taking time to find their feet and old campaigners like Ball, Simpson, Kelly and then current assistant manager at Highbury Pat Rice were beginning to wind down illustrious careers.

It was at this crossroads that a City side with a complete inability to win away from home arrived in North London one sunny autumn afternoon. In truth, the Blues were also in a transitional stage, as the great early 1970s side gave way to another tremendous team packed with talent towards the end of the decade. The new side was still a year away from gelling into the team that would eventually run Liverpool close for the league title.

While the likes of Mike Doyle, Alan Oakes and Colin Bell remained, City fans now sang the praises of Dave Watson, Asa Hartford and Dennis Tueart, too. City had already lost 2–0 at Coventry, 1–0 at West Ham, 1–0 at Derby and, in the interests of consistency, 1–0 at Aston Villa by the time this autumnal fixture arrived and were carrying a burgeoning reputation as the division's best home side – but they also possessed one of the worst away records. The previous midweek fixture had seen an away win of sorts, however. This had happened most unexpectedly at Stamford Bridge, but in a game against Norwich City during a second replay in the League Cup. A stunning 6–1 mauling of the Canaries which included a fine hat-trick from Dennis Tueart, gave the Blues the confidence they needed going to a ground where they habitually lost. Without a solitary away goal all season in the league, City surprised even their own supporters at Highbury by racing into a three-goal lead before the second half was two minutes old. With thoughts of win bonuses and adulatory press reports beginning to occupy the players' minds, things then took a change for the worse and, by the end, the Blues were doggedly hanging on for a 3–2 victory. It was ever thus.

This absorbing game centred on two titanic struggles in the middle of the park, which would eventually settle the match in City's favour. The first was between Ball and Doyle. Doyle enthused afterwards in typical fashion, 'It was nothing!' while Ball, still limping an hour after the game had ended said, 'I heard a thump, felt a thud and thought that my leg was broken!' The second, between the young Brady and the wily Hartford, raged all afternoon, culminating in a booking for the City midfielder. By then Hartford had already got his name on the scoresheet and Brady's role had become somewhat peripheral to proceedings.

City sparked into action first, Rodney Marsh and Willie Donachie linking well down the left flank. Bell's far-post flick was headed goalwards by Hartford, who saw his first effort saved by the stretching Jimmy Rimmer. The City man made no mistake with his second bite, tucking the ball away under the crossbar. City took the game beyond the Gunners with two rapid-fire goals either side of half time, the first something of a collector's item, a 25-yard rocket by Joe Royle and the second an ungainly side header by Marsh from Bell's accurate pass.

With City still busy congratulating themselves on this decisive change of fortune, Ball pulled one back from 20 yards out (his leg still working at this point). Arsenal then played out the rest of the game by laying siege to the City goal. Brady's effort was disallowed before Ball sent Alex Cropley though to jink the ball past the diving Corrigan. With Paul Power on for the injured Tueart, City managed to steady the ship and held out for the win. The effect on City's away fortunes was also interesting, as a string of score draws replaced the earlier defeats and an emphatic 4–0 win at Wolves, involving a comedy goal as players and referee fell over each other, underlined the point that City's away hoodoo had been well and truly put to bed at Highbury. Or so we all thought . . .

29 Pensioned Off

CHELSEA 1, CITY 4
DATE: 16 SEPTEMBER 1978
COMPETITION: DIVISION ONE
CITY: CORRIGAN, DONACHIE, POWER, VILJOEN, WATSON, P. FUTCHER,
CHANNON, OWEN, R. FUTCHER, HARTFORD, BARNES SUB: HENRY
ATTENDANCE: 29,980

Where was the author? Sick with 'flu watching Grandstand.

City went into the 1978/9 season attempting to keep up an increasingly high standard. The previous five seasons had seen finishes of 14th, 8th, 8th, 2nd and 4th and the Blues were now established as regular league title challengers with a big, expensively assembled squad and expectations to match. Despite an August Maine Road drubbing from Liverpool (this a regular occurrence whatever City's form), the Blues found themselves reasonably placed in tenth after the first five games had been played. They approached a tricky trip to Stamford Bridge on the back of an encouraging midweek draw in Enschede in the UEFA Cup.

Chelsea, still looking for a home goal and a home point, looked ripe for the picking – and so it would prove. The scene was set and, for Ron Futcher in particular, it was to be a great day, especially in his short and otherwise uneventful City career. Seen as padding in the £350,000 transfer that took his brother Paul from Luton Town to Maine Road, Ron was viewed primarily as the insurance policy, brought along to keep his brother from being homesick, while Paul was the England centre half in-waiting.

It had been the same story when they set off for Luton from Chester together and now brother Paul commanded more than two-thirds of the huge transfer fee that had brought them back north. Thanks to an injury to Brian Kidd, however, both brothers would play in this game and it would be Ron who would emerge the star turn. The great delight of visiting the capital and coming away with the points could be seen in every City fan's face on that bright sunny September afternoon in 1978. City came out wearing the 1970s classic white away kit with the black and red diagonal sash, itself in those days a hark back to the early '70s when City set the sartorial pace with a succession of similarly avant-garde kits.

With the midfield trio of Gary Owen, Asa Hartford and Colin Viljoen taking the game by the scruff of the neck right from the start, the crowd did not have long to wait for the first goal. Viljoen lifted a clever ball

Gary Owen played his part in the Blues' 4–1 win at Stamford Bridge in 1978.

over the statuesque home defence for Channon to run on to and slot past Peter Bonetti.

City were knocking the ball around with exhibition-match composure and Hartford rattled a post before the second goal arrived on 40 minutes. Joe Corrigan's prodigious punt downfield was carried on by the gusting wind, found Channon's head and thereafter Ron Futcher, who sliced through the remnants of the defence and tucked away a neat right-foot shot for his first ever City goal.

With Chelsea's demoralised players looking to the tunnel for half-time resuscitation, Futcher pounced again after 44 minutes. Started by his brother Paul's nippy defending, the move gained momentum through midfield thanks to the willing Hartford, who passed on to Channon. Finding Ron Futcher once again in space, the lanky striker stepped forward and hit an accurate shot past the 'keeper with his left foot.

It was not long into the second half before City had worked a fourth. Barnes whipped in a corner, which was not properly cleared. Hartford picked up the loose ball and angled it back into the box, where Ron Futcher stooped to head his hat-trick goal. This was not just any old treble, either, but the textbook classic of right foot, left foot, header.

City seemed to declare at four, letting the home side into the game more and Corrigan was forced to earn his salt with a number of saves, before a header from Gary Stanley crept past him after hitting the post. Chelsea left the field heads bowed, as Ron Futcher left the pitch, for once, the name on everyone's lips. He would finish the season with seven goals from ten starts – a more than fair return – before heading off to America in April 1979 to join Minnesota Kicks. It's doubtful anything ever topped this match in a career that faded into obscurity as the years went on.

30   The Match of the Decade?

CITY 5, TOTTENHAM HOTSPUR 2
DATE: 22 OCTOBER 1994
COMPETITION: PREMIERSHIP
CITY: DIBBLE, EDGHILL, CURLE, BRIGHTWELL, PHELAN, FLITCROFT,
LOMAS, SUMMERBEE, BEAGRIE, QUINN, WALSH
ATT: 25,473

Where was the author? In a hotel in Madeley, Staffordshire, about to ask Sarah to be my wife. Trust me to get the weekends wrong!

As the players trooped off the Maine Road pitch at the end of this rain-lashed game, John Motson declared to the watching *Match of the Day* millions that this had been one of the best games he could remember covering for BBC television. 'This was a throwback to how the game used to be played,' he commented as Maine Road stood and clapped to a man. For those lucky enough to be in the ground that day – the old ground's capacity had been severely reduced owing to the rebuilding of the Kippax – it would be a game that would live long in the memory.

Spurs, under Ossie Ardiles, were as committed to attacking football as City under Brian Horton and the match proved to be a monument to the respective managers' principles. In unrelenting rain, the ebb and flow of the first half produced four goals and a welter of untaken chances. City struck first as a right-wing cross was half cut out by a young Sol Campbell after 16 minutes, but, as the defender lost his bearings, Paul Walsh nipped in and tucked the ball away low to 'keeper Ian Walker's left-hand side.

Spurs were busy weaving intricate patterns through midfield and one of the more incisive of these allowed Jurgen Klinsmann to slip past the City defence, where he was unceremoniously upended by Andy Dibble, who had been sent off the week before for a similar kamikaze challenge on Les Ferdinand at QPR. Dibble survived with a yellow card and Romanian international Ilie Dumitrescu slotted the penalty away easily for the equaliser.

Before the break City had tied the game up, however, and went in 3–1 up thanks to the wing-play of Nicky Summerbee and, in particular, Peter Beagrie. First Summerbee's perfectly flighted right-wing cross was headed goalwards by Paul Walsh, only for Walker to parry his effort out to Niall Quinn. The big Irishman nodded home from a prone position, risking injury from Scott's flailing boot for his sixth goal in six games.

Then Beagrie skipped past two defenders on the left, motored over the halfway line and passed inside to Quinn, who moved the ball on in one movement to the incoming Walsh. The momentum of his shot carried the ball into the net after Walker's half-save. With the crowd – and John Motson – buzzing, the half-time whistle came as a rude intrusion on a superb spell of open football.

Nobody should have worried unduly about that, however, as the two sides resumed this pleasing spectacle immediately after the break. With just 60 seconds of the second period played, Dumitrescu rolled in a second Spurs goal from Klinsmann's clever backheel and the game was on a knife-edge once again. City charged back and, with Walsh weaving in and out on the left and Beagrie tormenting the Tottenham rearguard, the Blues managed to plunder two more goals. Beagrie, at his irrepressible best, left David Kerslake tackling fresh air before whipping in a cross that was headed home powerfully by Steve Lomas and then Walsh, enjoying his best game in City colours, set up Garry Flitcroft for the fifth. He ran at the heart of the Spurs rearguard, drawing three defenders in the process before laying the ball off to Flitcroft who finished with a clinical drive past Walker.

More chances came and went, but by this time the crowd was simply lapping up the one-touch football and basking in a performance that would warm the wet souls on the way home. Although Brian Horton's side would never quite reach these heights again, a swashbuckling 4–3 win at QPR in the League Cup followed the Spurs win and Ardiles lost his job shortly after the Maine Road drubbing.

Walsh would later claim he'd been spurred on by revenge over his former employers and his boss Horton said, 'The real winners were the paying public and the viewers around the world who watched the match on television. You won't see a better game of soccer than that. There were great individual performances from players on both sides. It wasn't all about Paul Walsh because there were tremendous performances from players like Peter Beagrie and Stevie Lomas. But you cannot take it away from Walsh. Even as a kid he had a great heart but I don't think he has ever played better in his career than he has since the day he arrived at Maine Road. All credit to Spurs. They didn't try to shut up shop and stop us playing. They kept going forward looking for goals just like us.'

31   The Keegan Factor

CITY 3, WATFORD 0
DATE: 11 AUGUST 2001
COMPETITION: DIVISION ONE
CITY: NASH, CHARVET, HOWEY, PEARCE, DUNNE, WIEKENS, GRANVILLE,
TIATTO, BERKOVIC, GOATER, WANCHOPE
ATTENDANCE: 33,939

---

*Where was the author? Sitting in the press box for the first time as editor
of the official club mag. I jumped up when we scored, banged my head
on the wooden cover and watched as hundreds of flecks of white paint
dropped on the other (unimpressed) journalists' heads – did I care? No!*

His mother 'warned him not to go near the main road,' so Kevin
Keegan informed the nation's media at his unveiling press
conference, but for the first couple of years of his reign as
Manchester City manager, the Blues' supporters were overjoyed he had.
His first competitive game was always going to be an electrically charged
affair, and so it proved in a cracking game that few who witnessed it
will ever forget. It was the start of a new, exciting era, with John Wardle
and David Makin's financial backing and one of the country's most
charismatic men at the helm. Heady days indeed, and not unlike the
movie *The Truman Show*, people wondered how it would all end.

Only two of Keegan's new boys started, but both Stuart Pearce and Eyal
Berkovic would have a major influence on a game that crackled with
expectancy from start to finish. The unusual Saturday evening kick-off
seemed to play its part, too, with ITV Digital choosing to have the match
start just as the other First Division fixtures finished, though with 4–0
victories for both Millwall and Bradford, plus a 5–0 win for Gillingham, it
was unlikely the Blues would finish the day as the league leaders.

With Maine Road rocking in the dusk and the floodlights gleaming
onto a perfect pitch, City and Watford walked out to a deafening roar
and Keegan took his place on the bench, waving to all four sides of the
ground as the people of Manchester welcomed the man charged with
waking a slumbering giant.

Playing a 5-3-2 formation, Carlo Nash got the nod in goal with
Laurent Charvet and Stuart Pearce the full-backs. A trio of experienced
centre-halves – Richard Dunne, Steve Howey and Gerard Wiekens –
completed the defence. Danny Tiatto, Danny Granville – both full-backs
in their own right – flanked Eyal Berkovic in midfield and Paulo
Wanchope and Shuan Goater were the strikers.

Watford, then under former Chelsea idol Gianluca Vialli's control, had arrived to spoil the party, but it quickly became clear that it was going to take a mammoth effort to repel the wave of optimism sweeping around the ground, backed up by a fluidity not seen for a number of years as the Blues launched a wave of attacks, almost exclusively prompted by the impressive Berkovic. Somehow, Watford survived until the break with the score still at 0–0. Their plan, whatever it was, was working and if they could survive an hour without conceding, they had a real chance of heading south with more than just a point.

Shaun Goater scored 31 goals during Kevin Keegan's first season (2001/2).

They were just two minutes away from the hour-mark when Charvet picked up Berkovic's clever ball on the right, sent over a delicious cross for Goater to crash home a header and send Maine Road wild. The Blues had their tails up now and tore mercilessly at Watford's beleaguered rear-guard. Just five minutes later Wanchope crashed a header against the bar and Berkovic collected the rebound, and cleverly moved the ball around Ramon Vega before planting the ball past Espen Baardsen for the second, killer goal. Berkovic whipped off his shirt and ran to his adoring new army of fans. It was fairytale stuff.

After Paul Robinson had been shown a second yellow card for Watford, Berkovic was substituted to a rapturous standing ovation on 76 minutes – but there was still one more chapter to be written on what was a magical evening for City fans. With just a few minutes left on the clock, the Blues won a free-kick on the edge of the box. If the script was to be followed to the letter, Stuart Pearce needed to take it and score one of those trademark howitzers that was his speciality at Nottingham Forest. Pearce did step up – and did score with a thunderous free-kick. It really was the perfect end to a perfect start for Keegan and his new side.

'It was a tremendous performance,' he said afterwards. 'We didn't get our rewards in the first half – but the lads kept their heads down and the football we played was breathtaking. But I think we can play better.'

They did, too, but the atmosphere and raw passion of that opening game was never bettered.

32 Dennis the Menace

City 6, Chelsea 2
Date: 26 November 1977
Competition: Division One
City: Corrigan, Clements, Donachie, Booth, Watson, Barnes, Channon, Tueart, Kidd, Hartford, Power
Attendance: 34,345

Where was the author? Painting my mum's bathroom while listening to Brian Clarke's updates.

City went into this game in patchy form to say the least. Five defeats in the previous eight games had left the Blues slightly adrift of the pace, having led the table going into October with five wins and two draws from the opening seven games. It was a time of transition, with Joe Royle loaned to Bristol City and making his debut the same day, Dennis Tueart, unhappy at being in and out of the side, was on the transfer list and Colin Bell still absent with injury.

Having beaten Manchester United, Liverpool and Arsenal at Maine Road already, newly promoted Chelsea presented the perfect opportunity to get the season back on track. Oddly, the crowd was well below the 45,000 average with just over 34,000 turning up for what was destined to be a cracking afternoon's entertainment. The Chelsea contingent, however, tucked away in the top right-hand corner of the Kippax, would soon be wishing they'd stayed home and kept warm.

It would be a day the Pensioners' full-back Graham Wilkins would remember for a long time, too, and he began his hour of misery by putting through his own net to give City the lead on nine minutes. Four minutes later Tueart made it 2–0, with the Blues hardly even breaking into a sweat.

Tony Book urged his side to put Chelsea to the sword, but, in a surprising twist, Graham Wilkins pulled one back for the visitors and, from being seemingly down and out, on 27 minutes, Kenny Clements gave a penalty away that allowed Ian Britton to level the scores at 2–2. City were far from finished, however, and despite Chelsea's tail wagging, an air of apprehension settled over Maine Road – but it only lasted four minutes as Tueart scored his second of the afternoon on 31 minutes. City began to pummel Chelsea with Asa Hartford and Peter Barnes outstanding. Paul Power's low drive struck John Sparrow and spun towards the opposite corner to Peter 'The Cat' Bonetti and the former England 'keeper could

City boss Tony Book came close to guiding the Blues to the title in 1977 and 1978.

only watch helplessly as the ball rolled over the line to make it 4–2 on half time.

Barnes continued to terrorise the hapless Wilkins after the break and on 51 minutes the Kippax idol made it 5–2 with a classy finish that secured the points for the Blues. In fact, Wilkins, thoroughly fed up with his lot and chasing shadows all afternoon, fouled Barnes repeatedly, eventually giving referee McNally no option but to send him for an early bath. Tueart then completed his hat-trick (his second of the season) on 69 minutes to make it 6–2. With more than 20 minutes remaining, the City fans wondered just how big the final winning margin might be, but the Blues eased their foot off the gas and there was no more scoring. Buoyed with confidence, City won their next six successive home games, Bell returned from injury and, for a few weeks, all was well with the world. Tueart claimed after the game that his treble changed nothing and he was better off finding a new home. He scored one more hat-trick before he left for New York Cosmos early in the New Year.

Everton also hit six the day City hammered Chelsea, beating Coventry 6–0 and Joe Royle marked his Bristol City debut by scoring all four goals in a 4–1 win over Middlesbrough. As for Chelsea, they clawed back a little pride by holding the Blues to a 0–0 draw in the return fixture at Stamford Bridge.

33   One For The Road

Tottenham Hotspur 1, City 3
Date: 4 May 1968
Competition: Division One
City: Mulhearn, Book, Pardoe, Doyle, Heslop, Oakes, Lee, Bell, Summerbee, Young, Coleman
Attendance: 51,242

Where was the author? Too young to know what was going on!

Maximum points from the final two games of the season and the championship would be coming back to Maine Road for the first time since 1937. There was no room for error with Manchester United on the same points – but with a worse goal average – and the Blues knew any slip-ups would probably be punished by their neighbours.

Tottenham hadn't lost to City at White Hart Lane since 1960 and had their own agenda of finishing in sixth position to attend to – a win would virtually guarantee them ending the season as the top club in London. Plus Spurs had finished third the previous campaign and with 51,242 fans packed into the Lane, Joe Mercer's side knew they'd have to perform to their optimum level to leave with both points in the bag.

Mercer was at least able to pick his strongest team for the third successive game and the starting eleven that ran out had played together as a unit on sixteen occasions that season and been beaten just once, winning eleven and drawing the other four.

Skipper Tony Book recalls how the team were feeling prior to kick-off, 'We were really fired up for this game – we knew that two more wins and we were champions and White Hart Lane felt like a happy hunting ground and fortunately, we gave one of our best displays of the season.'

Spurs had the prolific Jimmy Greaves up front and were at full strength too, but it was the Blues who came storming out of the blocks, pinning the hosts back for long periods with some sparkling passing and clean, crisp tackling.

'Spurs had a damned good side and we knew we had to go for their throats straight from the kick-off,' recalled City legend Mike Doyle. 'They hade Martin Chivers, a big, strong forward and their famous old warhorse Dave Mackay to contend with in the middle of the park and Jimmy Greaves was banging in goals for fun, yet in those first 30 minutes, I don't think Spurs had a single shot. We were going for it hell-for-leather and every City player seemed to give two hundred per cent. We played Spurs

Mike Summerbee always enjoyed playing Spurs, but particularly in 1967/8 when he scored in both league games and generally tormented the North London side in each match.

off the park and Colin Bell gave one of the finest displays I've ever seen, that day.'

With 40 minutes of an incredibly tense game gone, the one thing City hadn't done was score – until the magnificent Bell struck to send the travelling fans wild. It was the perfect time to score and was enough to take the visitors into the break 1–0 up.

Mercer and Malcolm Allison knew Spurs would come back strongly after the break so the dream scenario was, of course, to kill the game off as quickly possible and within a minute of the restart Bell had made it 2–0 to give the Blues vital breathing space. It was just as well because Spurs piled on the pressure from then on and the efforts of the first half – and an epic season – began to show.

Had the hosts, who hit the woodwork twice, taken any of their numerous chances, it would have been a severe test of City's durability, but, in the style of a great side, they soaked up as much as Spurs could throw at them, broke downfield and, with 74 minutes on the clock, went 3–0 up through Mike Summerbee.

With the wind knocked out of their sails, Spurs' only riposte was a Jimmy Greaves penalty on 83 minutes following a George Heslop hand-ball, but it was too little, too late. One more win and the title would be City's.

34   The Demolition Derby

CITY 4, MANCHESTER UNITED 0
DATE: 15 NOVEMBER 1969
COMPETITION: DIVISION ONE
CITY: CORRIGAN, BOOK, PARDOE, DOYLE, HESLOP (TOWERS), OAKES,
SUMMERBEE, BELL, LEE, MANN, JEFFRIES
ATTENDANCE: 63,013

Where was the author? Asleep in bed, aged 2!

They called it one of the most one-sided derby matches ever – a massacre, in fact – and one the majority of the 63,000 crowd never forgot. The news reports commented on the 'vast gulf between two ill-matched sides' and of it being 'manna from heaven for Blues fans'. City went into the match having failed to beat United at Maine Road since September 1959, but in good form in the league having lost just one of their previous thirteen games.

Both sides were still attempting to get back on the rails having both endured a mediocre 1968/9 campaign while, in City's case, defending the title, and in United's, the European Cup. While the Blues were riding high, the Reds were clearly going through something of a transitional period.

With the teams due to meet again in a two-legged League Cup semi-final just a few weeks later, it was important to gain an edge to take into those games and it was United who came desperately close to opening the scoring in the first minute, with Denis Law just failing to connect with John Aston's inviting ball across the box. Had that gone in, who knows which way the game might have swung? As it was, the Blues heeded the warning and effortlessly slipped up a gear from that moment on, though it wasn't until the 38th minute that the hosts finally went in front.

Neil Young had been fairly quiet up to that point, but when he received the ball within sight of goal, he feigned to cross but instead sent in a wicked curling drive that totally fooled Alex Stepney and flew into the back of the net.

With just one goal separating the sides at the break, the Reds could have been forgiven for thinking they had a good shot at clawing their way back into the match, but 10 minutes after half time, the peerless Colin Bell doubled City's advantage to make it 2–0. United's talismanic trio of Bobby Charlton, Law and George Best were powerless to prevent the relentless wave of attacks, led by man-of-the-match Bell, and when the Blues went 3–0 up, courtesy of an own goal, the Kippax began to enjoy the occasion, safe in the knowledge that there was no way back for Sir Matt's boys.

Joe Corrigan watches on as his City team-mates dismantle United in 1969.

Mike Summerbee, Franny Lee, Young and Bell had attacked from the front throughout with a mixture of flair and aggression and United had, quite simply, been overwhelmed. Alan Oakes, Glyn Pardoe, Tony Book and, of course, Mike Doyle, played like men inspired and nobody was about to take their foot off the gas, least of all the majestic Bell who scrambled home a fourth on 89 minutes to complete United's nightmarish afternoon.

Malcolm Allison had instilled a real belief within his troops that United were nothing to be scared of – he'd told them to go out prior to derbies at Old Trafford and walk in front of the Stretford End, effectively taking the fear away, and the move paid instant dividends with successive wins at United in 1968 and 1969 and, once again, that helped the Blues triumph again a few weeks later, beating the Reds 2–1 in the first leg of the League Cup semi-final and drawing 2–2 in the return.

Oddly, with many expecting City to make a genuine challenge for the title following the demolition derby, Joe Mercer's side won just one of their next twelve games and would actually finish below United in the table. On the plus side, City completed a league double over the Reds and won the League Cup against West Brom a few months later. Oh, and won the European Cup Winners' Cup, too. It wasn't such a bad season after all. . .

35 Villa Spark

ASTON VILLA 1, CITY 4
DATE: 24 AUGUST 1977
COMPETITION: DIVISION ONE
CITY: CORRIGAN, CLEMENTS, DONACHIE, DOYLE, WATSON, BOOTH,
KIDD, CHANNON, ROYLE, HARTFORD, TUEART
ATTENDANCE: 40,121

Where was the author? Frustrated at home having seen my first match just four days earlier – a boring 0–0 with Leicester City – but I was hooked!

Just a few months earlier, City had missed out on the title by a solitary point to Liverpool, effectively changing the club's destiny over the next twenty years, though nobody knew as much at the time. Had the Blues taken the title, who knows how they would have fared in the European Cup? They may have ducked out in the first round – there were no lucrative group stages back in the 1970s – or they might have gone on to win it and gone from strength to strength as a result of the cash windfall that would accompanied such success. One thing was for sure, there was enough talent in Tony Book's side to have achieved anything they wanted to, with a little rub of the green – and a fit Colin Bell.

Only Mike Channon had been added to the side that narrowly finished runners-up, with the England international signing from Southampton for a club record fee of £300,000 and City were again among the favourites for the title, as were their opponents Aston Villa. The Blues went into the second game of the 1977/8 campaign on the back of a disappointing 0–0 draw at home to Leicester City. Gary Owen was dropped in favour of Brian Kidd and the teams ran out to a packed Villa Park on a damp Wednesday evening in the Midlands.

Former Blues manager Ron Saunders was now in charge at Villa and, ironically, his last act as City boss had been to sign Dennis Tueart from Sunderland – it's a fair bet he wished he'd never even heard of Tueart by the time this game had finished. Villa roared out of the blocks, intent on giving a noisy, partisan crowd exactly what they wanted and with just four minutes gone, John Deehan put the ball past Joe Corrigan to put Saunders' side ahead. It was just the start Book didn't want. Yet just two minutes later, it was the travelling supporters going wild as Tommy Booth headed home the equaliser. It had been an exhilarating start and the next goal would be crucial – and both teams went at each other hammer and tongs. Villa should have retaken the lead when Alex Cropley was twice presented with superb opportunities to put the hosts back in front within the space of four minutes, but he spurned both to the dismay of the expectant masses.

Those misses seemed to sow a seed of doubt into the Villa players' minds and on 28 minutes, Tueart scored his first of the night, recreating his spectacular League Cup Final winner by scoring with an overhead kick from Mike Doyle's throw-in. It was typical of Tueart to conjure something out of nothing and if the Blues were serious in their title aspirations, they needed players of Tueart's calibre who could turn the tide their way when things were tight.

There were no further goals in the first period and the players were greeted by a torrential downpour after the break, with Book asking for 'more of the same' from his players. City looked slick, their passing zipped around the greasy surface while Villa's threat was occasional but not constant and when they did break through, they were met by the sight of the man-mountain Corrigan who was at his imperious best. Booth, Doyle and Dave Watson were magnificent at the back and the home team's will began to weaken as it became clear the Blues had too much quality and were hell-bent on returning north with all three points. It wasn't until the final six minutes, however, that the City fans could relax when on 84 minutes, Tueart took advantage of some hesitant defending to make it 3–1.

Three minutes later, Tueart was celebrating his first away hat-trick after Kenny Clements' long clearance left him through on goal. As former Manchester United 'keeper Jimmy Rimmer ran out, Tueart chipped it over his head to complete an emphatic 4–1 win in style. It had been a fantastic night for City, and Tueart in particular, who went on to score two more hat-tricks that season. The Villa Park win was the Blues' best performance on the road that season and the victory prmised another assault on the league title, though ultimately, Book's side had to settle for fourth position.

36   Who's Afraid of the Big Bad Wolves?

Manchester City 5, Wolverhampton Wanderers 2
Date: 29 January 1972
Competition: Division One
City: Corrigan, Book, Donachie, Doyle, Booth, Oakes,
Summerbee (Hill 60), Bell, Davies, Lee, Towers
Attendance: 37,639

Where was the author? Playing in the backyard, most likely.

G oing into game 29 of the 1971/2 campaign, City had lost only four games all season. The defeats came against sides the Blues traditionally struggled against – Leeds United (twice), Derby County and Wolverhampton Wanderers with the latter the opponents on a dull, cold Saturday afternoon at Maine Road. The teams had already shared a goal-feast earlier in the campaign with City edging a seven-goal thriller in a League Cup second-round clash back in September, so the hardy souls who shivered away on the Kippax for this game at least felt there was a chance of an entertaining afternoon ahead.

Franny Lee was in white-hot form having already bagged twenty goals going into this match and his partnership with Wyn Davies was proving irresistible. Tony Towers was in the form of his life and Joe Mercer only changed his starting line-up when absolutely necessary – just like the 1967/8 championship season, the team-sheet rarely changed and there was a real belief the Blues could bring the title back to Maine Road again.

With former Kippax idol Dave Wagstaffe making a welcome return in the gold and black of Wolves, who themselves were in sparkling form and making a determined surge up the First Division table, City immediately took the game to the visitors. With Stan Gibson's pitch reduced to a cabbage patch with the odd blade of grass here and there, the ball was never going to move around the surface smoothly and both teams adopted a more direct approach. The Blues, however, stole a march after just five minutes when Tommy Booth rose to put his team 1–0 up and on 24 minutes Lee scored his twenty-first of the season to seemingly put the hosts in the box-seat.

But as dangerous as City were, there was a frailty about the home defence that Wolves sensed. Joe Corrigan didn't seem to be at the races and his defenders were hardly watertight – it was seven games since they collectively kept a clean sheet and on 34 minutes, the visitors' probing was rewarded when the prolific John Richards pulled a goal back.

That seemed to wake City, and within six minutes Towers had restored the Blues' two-goal advantage by scoring a third – a lead the hosts took into the half-time break. Yet whatever Mercer and Malcolm Allison said to the side as they sipped their tea in the dressing room, it didn't work immediately as Richards again brought Wolves back into the game with his second of the afternoon coming just six minutes after the restart.

It was proving an absorbing clash, perhaps even more so because the Blues were aware that if results went their way, they would go into February as the league leaders. On the hour, the impressive Mike Summerbee limped off and substitute Freddie Hill climbed off the bench for his first appearance of the season – and it was Hill who changed the sway of the game, too, adding a new dimension to City's midfield that had strangely lacked spark, mainly due to Colin Bell having a rare off-day.

The next goal was going to be critical – if it went the way of City, surely there would be no way back for the visitors. If Wolves levelled, however, they would likely go on and clinch both points – after all, they had already scored three times at Maine Road on one occasion that season. Fortunately, super-sub Hill proved to be the catalyst for the Blues to push on and eventually win at a canter. His back-headed flick from Bell's cross landed perfectly for Lee to crack home City's fourth just past the hour-mark allowing a nervy Maine Road to settle and enjoy the last third of the game and Lee provided the perfect *coup de grâce* by completing his hat-trick with two minutes to go.

With a 5–2 home win in the bank, City smoothly moved into the pole position with just fourteen games to go. Even during a patchy performance they had proved they had sufficient gears to ease past tricky opposition – the title beckoned . . . at least until Malcolm Allison decided on bringing the enigmatic Rodney Marsh to Maine Road for the final few furlongs.

37   Belgian Waffle

CITY 5, SK LIERSE 0
DATE: 26 NOVEMBER 1969
COMPETITION: EUROPEAN CUP WINNERS' CUP ROUND 2, 2ND LEG
CITY: MULHEARN, BOOK, PARDOE, DOYLE, BOOTH, OAKES, SUMMERBEE
(HILL), BELL, BOWYER (TOWERS), LEE, JEFFRIES
ATTENDANCE: 34,345

*Where was the author? Not sure, but probably asleep or annoying my
brother and sister.*

The now-defunct European Cup Winners' Cup consisted of just 32
clubs when the Blues entered the competition as FA Cup holders
in the 1969/70 season. Four aggregate victories would send two
clubs all the way to the final in Vienna, though the pedigree of the
teams competing was obviously high. For the sake of younger readers,
the ECWC was a tournament solely for teams who had won domestic
competitions across Europe with England's only representatives being
the FA Cup holders (winning the League Cup didn't merit European
qualification at the time).

Koninklijke Lierse Sportkring – better known as SK Lierse – were
a part-time outfit from Belgium who weren't expected to progress too
far in the competition, but they had seen off Cypriot side APOEL in the
previous round, winning the home leg 10–1, so they were no patsies.
Still, City eased through the first leg with a 3–0 win in Belgium making
the return game at Maine Road seemingly nothing more than a formality;
however the opening exchanges proved to be anything but.

Lierse came at City a dangerous beast – they had nothing to lose at all
and should have been 2–0 up inside the opening 15 minutes. Had they
taken their chances, the Blues just might have been on the end of the
most dramatic turnaround in the history of European club competition.
Lierse striker De Nul was causing no end of problems and had one
effort scrambled off the line and he then hit the post with a snap shot
out of nothing, with Ken Mulhearn well-beaten. The Belgians had clearly
understood their manager's instructions to throw caution to the wind and
see where it took them and their brave approach earned the respect of a
half-full Maine Road.

Freezing conditions had left the pitch rock hard and the Blues were
finding it difficult to get the ball on the ground and play their natural
passing game but, in true ballet on ice style, a change of footwear (this
time at the break), would prove the undoing of their opponents. Just three

Mike Doyle (centre), Franny Lee (left) and Neil Young (right) celebrate another goal during the run to the 1970 European Cup Winners' Cup Final.

minutes after the restart, Mike Summerbee blasted City ahead, ending any lingering hopes Lierse might have had of causing an upset. From then on, the Blues were in total control and Colin Bell and Francis Lee were particularly impressive, adding a goal each in quick succession to make it three goals in 12 minutes.

Youngster Derek Jeffries was making a good impression with his intelligent passing and technique standing out, but it was Bell and Lee who completed the rout, each scoring another goal to give City a 5–0 win on the night and 8–0 aggregate overall – a club record which still stands today. Lierse headed back to Belgium chastised, but with their heads held high having played their part in an absorbing European night.

38   Boxing Clever

CITY 8, SCUNTHORPE UNITED 1
DATE: 26 DECEMBER 1963
COMPETITION: DIVISION TWO
CITY: DOWD, BETTS, SEAR, KENNEDY, WOOD, OAKES, YOUNG, GRAY,
MURRAY, KEVAN, WAGSTAFFE
ATTENDANCE: 26,365

Where was the author? Still not born.

The Blues went into the 1963/4 season having been relegated the season before. Despite ending Tottenham's title hopes with a 1–0 win at Maine Road three games before the end of a miserable campaign, a 1–1 draw with Manchester United sent City tumbling out of the top flight for the first time since 1951. Even more galling was the fact that the point ensured United's survival and City and Leyton Orient, who'd been relegated a month earlier, left Division One. Long-serving manager Les McDowall had left the club after thirteen years in charge and his final game was a 6–1 defeat at West Ham, further rubbing salt into the Blues' wounds and taking the goals conceded tally to 102!

For the new campaign, new boss George Poyser signed Derek Kevan from Chelsea as well as adding Jimmy Murray from Wolves in November. Along with Matt Gray, plus Neil Young and Dave Wagstaffe on the flanks, the Blues possessed one of the most lethal attacks in the division and were tipped by many to make a quick return to the top league, though with the likes of Leeds United and Sunderland to contend with (both of whom narrowly missed out on promotion the previous season), it was going to be a tough ask.

The first half of the campaign would be one of few highs, though the 3–2 win over Leeds at Maine Road was one of them. The Blues had started promisingly with seven points from a possible ten and Kevan proved an instant success with five goals in five games, but just one win in the next nine saw Poyser's side plummet down the table while both Leeds and Sunderland kicked on, opening up a gap of several points.

Jimmy Murray had scored on his debut for City in a 4–2 defeat at Southampton and another loss, this time away to Newcastle United, had the pundits writing off the Blues by the end of autumn – and rightly so, six wins, five draws and seven defeats as the halfway mark approached meant just 17 points had been amassed from a possible 36. However, Murray's arrival was about to give City renewed hope and a 5–2 home win over Huddersfield was followed with a 2–0 win away to Leyton

The prolific Derek Kevan, scorer of two goals in City's 8–1 Boxing Day win over Scunthorpe United in 1963.

Orient. As the festive programme approached, the Blues took a useful point in a 2–2 draw at Portsmouth and followed it up with their last game before Christmas in emphatic style – a 6–1 victory over a decent Rotherham United team meant the home match in the double-header against struggling Scunthorpe United on Boxing Day could be another chance for the Blues to add to their impressive goals tally. Since Murray's arrival, City had scored eighteen goals in just six games and Murray had helped himself to eight of them – a fantastic return.

As the country settled down for Christmas Day, Poyser plotted the downfall of the Iron as his Christmas dinner settled and a chilly Maine Road opened its gates the following day for an expectant crowd of 26,365 – the second highest of the season. But for 40 minutes, Scunthorpe gave as good as they got, keeping the country's most prolific strike force at bay. However, they finally succumbed to the constant home attacks and inevitably it was Murray who opened the scoring, just before the break. Whatever George Poyser said to his misfiring troops during the half-time cuppa certainly worked, as the Blues shifted up several gears after the break. For the first time since the Second World War, City bagged seven goals in one half with Murray completing his second successive hat-trick and Matt Gray also hitting a treble. Kevan scored the other two in the 8–1 victory that firmly established the Blues as promotion hopefuls once again.

Two days later the exact same starting eleven beat a thoroughly demoralised Scunthorpe 4–2 at Glanford Park with Murray scoring two more to take his tally to thirteen in eight games. With 27 goals in six matches, Poyser's side were in white-hot form going into their top-of-the-table clashes with Leeds and Sunderland. Unfortunately, failure to win any of the next seven games meant the promotion dream was effectively over and the Blues eventually finished sixth with both Leeds and Sunderland winning promotion to the top flight. Still, what a Christmas it had been . . .

39   Final Replay

City 3, Gornik Zabrze 1
Date: 31 March 1971
Competition: European Cup Winners' Cup, 3rd Round (Replay)
City: Healey, Connor, Towers, Doyle, Booth, Donachie, Jeffries, Bell, Lee, Young, Hill
Attendance: 12,100

Where was the author? Reading a comic before bedtime.

In the league, City couldn't buy a goal and were in the middle of an atrocious run. One strike in eight games and seven blanks meant Joe Mercer's side were well out of the title race and Division One was proving extremely tight with everyone seemingly able to beat each other. Having ducked out of the FA Cup and League Cup, the European Cup Winners' Cup represented the only hope of a fourth successive season of landing silverware, but with the City strikers misfiring badly, it was hard to see where the goals would come from.

Having limped past part-timers Linfield and Honved in previous rounds, City were paired with their old foes Gornik Zabrze in the last eight for a repeat of the 1970 Cup Winners' Cup Final with the Poles determined to avenge the defeat in Vienna. The first leg for the out-of-sorts Blues was in Poland and with 100,000 fanatical fans screaming their heroes on, the hosts won 2–0.

Despite the odds being stacked against them, City triumphed 2–0 at Maine Road with goals from Mike Doyle and Ian Mellor levelling the aggregate score, but with no penalties to settle the tie, a replay in Copenhagen was organised for a week later. It was proving to be an expensive round for the loyal supporters who travelled over to Denmark to form part of the 12,100 crowd that also included many curious locals. Just eleven months earlier the Blues had faced Gornik on neutral soil and now the teams again locked horns for the right to face Chelsea in the semi-final. Mercer's team settled into the unfamiliar surroundings far quicker than Gornik did, and with Doyle marauding forward and roughing-up 'keeper Kostlea, Gornik looked vulnerable and, as a result, the first goal was born out of apprehension from the Polish custodian. Neil Young, with just one league goal all season, sent in a hopeful punt and Kostlea made a complete hash of his attempt to punch the ball clear and the ball trickled over the line, gifting the Blues a 1–0 lead. Gornik looked bereft of ideas and fell further behind when the impressive Tommy Booth headed home the second, killer goal for City.

Dave Connor – a hugely underrated defender who was an integral part of the Mercer-Allison era. He made four starts during the Blues' surge to the European Cup Winners' Cup semi-final in 1970/1.

The Poles did rally briefly and the dangerous Włodzimierz Lubański finally pulled one back on 57 minutes. Only a fantastic save by Ronnie Healey stopped Gornik levelling two minutes later. Fortunately, City still had plenty in reserve and when Colin Bell picked the ball up some 50 yards from goal, there seemed little threat to the Gornik defence, but 'Nijinsky' then burst forward and effortlessly glided past five players before slipping the ball to Franny Lee who tapped home a decisive third on 65 minutes. There was no further scoring and Mercer's side eased through 3–1 to book a two-legged semi-final with Chelsea a fortnight later. Gornik boss Ferenc Suzousa said afterwards, 'I hold my hands up, Manchester City were a mile better than us tonight. Now I wish them luck in their quest to retain the trophy.'

Unfortunately, injuries meant the first leg at Stamford Bridge was always going to be difficult and though a severely weakened City lost only 1–0, the second leg again showed the striking deficiencies of the Blues as they again lost 1–0 to exit the competition and complete a largely miserable season with no silverware to add the trophy cabinet.

As a footnote, Chelsea went on to play Real Madrid in the final in Athens and led 1–0 until the Spaniards equalised in the 90th minute. Two days later, Chelsea triumphed 2–1 over Madrid, so the trophy at least remained in England, though sadly not in Manchester.

40   Hit For Six

CITY 6, BLACKBURN 0
DATE: 17 SEPTEMBER 1983
COMPETITION: DIVISION TWO
CITY: WILLIAMS, RANSON, MAY, BOND, POWER, CATON, MCNAB, REID,
BAKER, TOLMIE, PARLANE (DAVIDSON)
ATTENDANCE: 34,345

*Where was the author? In the Platt Lane or Main Stand for this one – not
sure which, though.*

After suffering relegation on the final day of the 1982/3 campaign,
the Blues had to hit the ground running if they were to return to
the top flight at the first attempt. City's last game outside Division
One had been a 0–0 draw with Southampton back in May 1966 and
the fixture list for the 1983/4 campaign produced a myriad of clubs City
hadn't faced in league action for many years.

Destinations such as Cardiff, Grimsby, Charlton Athletic, Carlisle and
Cambridge all held novelty value, but little else. For a club City's size,
the need to win promotion at the first time of asking was critical, if for
financial reasons alone. The second tier of English football was littered
with 'sleeping giants' who were closer to being comatose after numerous
failed attempts to regain their lofty status and the Blues could ill-afford to
join that list.

Any league that included Chelsea, Leeds and Newcastle United was
going to be tough to escape from, but new manager Billy McNeill was
well aware of the task ahead and had recruited players he knew well
– mostly fellow Scots – who he felt could do a decent job. There was
hardly any transfer kitty to speak of, so Neil McNab, Jim Tolmie and
Derek Parlane were all brought in for under a total of £150,000, while
Joe Corrigan, Dennis Tueart, David Cross and Asa Hartford had all moved
on.

McNeill's new-look team had begun the season with a 2–0 win at
Crystal Palace but then lost 2–1 at Cardiff just two days later. A thrilling
3–2 victory over Barnsley suggested the Parlane/Tolmie partnership
could be particularly fruitful with pair already responsible for five of
the six goals scored so far. A frustrating 0–0 draw with Fulham was then
followed by a 2–1 win at Portsmouth – Tolmie and Parlane again scoring
the goals – which meant that the Blues ran out at Maine Road to face
Blackburn handily placed in fourth position.

Rovers had only lost one of their opening five games and had conceded just five goals in the process, so anything but an easy ride was expected by the 25,443 crowd – the third highest in the country that day.

City wore a Saab-sponsored all-sky blue kit with Rovers, backed by around 1,000 travelling fans, all in yellow. With the sun shining and the Kippax in good voice, the Blues were quick to force the issue and with just 11 minutes on the clock, Andy May put the hosts ahead with his second goal of the campaign – but there was much more to come. On 27 minutes, City went 2–0 up thanks to a cracking drive from Parlane who was quickly becoming a crowd favourite in the blue half of Manchester. The tall, former Leeds United and Rangers striker didn't do a great deal outside of the box, but in it, he looked a predator and though there was concern when he hobbled off for treatment on 35 minutes, he returned to put the game beyond doubt on 41 minutes when he made it 3–0 from close range.

City were rampant and Tolmie and Parlane looked as though they'd been playing alongside each other for years as the pair continued their scoring exploits after the break, with Parlane completing a 23-minute hat-trick on 50 minutes and Tolmie adding a fifth on 52 meaning they had now scored eleven of City's thirteen goals so far that season. McNeill must have been chuffed that his gamble on the pint-sized Tolmie was paying off. He'd paid Lokeren £30,000 to secure his services and this after Tolmie had failed to score in eighteen appearances for the Belgian side.

The twelve-time capped Parlane was less of a risk, even aged thirty, though his record at previous club Leeds United averaged one goal in every five matches. If McNeill was to guide City back to the First Division, he'd need Parlane and Tolmie to continue their rich vein of form throughout the season.

The Blues still had time to really rub Blackburn's noses in the mud with Baker adding a sixth before full-time. It was the biggest home win since Leyton Orient had been beaten by the same score in August 1964 and it pushed City into second place in the table, a point behind leaders Sheffield Wednesday. Three successive league wins followed to put McNeill's men at the division's summit, but the squad's frailties emerged as the months passed by and despite the Tolmie/Parlane partnership yielding a total of 34 goals, City finished in fourth position, 10 points adrift of third-placed Newcastle.

41   Barnes Stormer

Tottenham Hotspur 0, City 3
Date: 2 March 1979
Competition: Division One
City: Corrigan, Power, Donachie, P. Futcher, Watson (Deyna 45), Bell, Owen, Barnes, Hartford, Kidd, Channon
Attendance: 32,037

Where was the author? Yes, absent from another away game – just didn't have the money back then.

Malcolm Allison had been back at Maine Road for a matter of days and already City had been involved in various dramas of one kind or another. Having finished fourth the previous season, Tony Book's side was expected to push on and again challenge Liverpool for the title. Just two defeats in the opening nineteen league and cup matches suggested the Blues were again a force to be reckoned with.

But for some reason, from October until February, City couldn't buy a win in the league. Six draws and seven defeats – all by a single-goal margin – proved there wasn't a great deal wrong with Book's side, but for whatever reason, they couldn't quite get their act together and were slipping down the table at a steady if not dramatic rate. There was no doubting the quality of the team which was virtually the same eleven players who had pushed hard for the title for the previous two years, but something wasn't gelling.

The board, in their infinite wisdom, decided they needed a more charismatic face on the coaching team and decided to bring Malcolm Allison back as Book's right-hand man. The management change meant there was no room for the highly respected first team coach Bill Taylor, with the popular Scot shown the door at Maine Road – scandalously in many peoples' eyes.

Another potential problem with Allison's appointment was that his powerful character was bound to make Tony Book's life hard, and inevitably there would be questions asked as to who exactly was in charge. Book had played under Allison just six years earlier and now he was expected to tell his former gaffer what to do – it was a risky move to say the least and undermined Book's authority.

Initially, things seemed to be improving – a 1–1 draw at Leeds United was followed by a home game with Chelsea whom the Blues had already thrashed 4–1 at Stamford Bridge earlier in the campaign and goals from

Peter Barnes, stunning in the 3–0 win at Spurs but sacrificed by Malcolm Allison just a few months later along with another crowd favourite, Gary Owen.

Ron Futcher and Paul Power put City 2–0 up. It seemed the thirteen-game winless run was about to end – but the Pensioners scored three times to win the game 3–2 as the crisis deepened. Worse was to follow when Third-Division Shrewsbury Town knocked the Blues out of the FA Cup with a 2–0 win on a frozen Gay Meadow pitch.

With a trip to White Hart Lane next on the agenda, things looked as though they might get worse before they got better. Colin Bell returned to the team for only his second appearance of the season and was employed in a new sweeper role and the game was selected for ITV's *The Big Match*.

Spurs had their own problems, having failed to win any of their previous six league matches, so something had to give. It was clear the first goal was going to lift a huge weight off one team's shoulders and Spurs looked the more likely to break the deadlock. Steve Perryman burst from defence into the Blues' half and found himself with just Joe Corrigan to beat after Ossie Ardiles' chip was directed into his path, but he showed a defender's touch when he nudged the ball just enough for Corrigan to smother the opportunity.

Soon after, the hosts had a penalty claim turned down, and seconds later City took the lead. Peter Barnes was looking at his very best and when Gary Owen instinctively played the ball into his path, Perryman clipped Barnes' heels and the referee had no option but to award City a penalty. Brian Kidd stepped up to drive the ball past Mark Kendal and gave the Blues a priceless lead.

There was worse to follow for Spurs when Barnes, in electric form, skipped past three challenges before hammering a left-foot drive past Kendal to make it 2–0 before the break. Suddenly, City were oozing confidence and appeared to have rediscovered their early season form.

Peter Taylor volleyed over from close range before the break and an injury to Dave Watson meant the England defender was substituted at half time. Tottenham began the second half brightly but each time Corrigan thwarted their efforts and eventually City regained control. The goal of the game came on 75 minutes when Owen fed Barnes on the left – the flying winger skipped past McAllister as though he wasn't there, ghosted past another defender before picking out Mick Channon who made no mistake from close range. The linesman confused matters by attracting the referee's attention and it seemed the goal may have been ruled out, but it was merely to ensure McAllister was booked for trying to impede Barnes in the build-up to the goal.

As thousands drifted out of White Hart Lane, City comfortably played out the final moments to claim a fine victory.

42 Clarets Put To The Sword

City 5, Burnley 1
Date: 29 December 2001
Competition: Division One
City: Nash, Edghill, Mettomo, Wiekens (Dunne), Howey,
Horlock, Berkovic, Tiatto, Wanchope, Goater (Huckerby),
Benarbia (Wright-Phillips)
Attendance: 34,250

Where was the author? Seated in the lower tier of the Kippax

Burnley were the surprise package of the 2001/2 campaign and arrived at Maine Road for the final game of the year four points clear of second-placed City at the top of Division One. The Blues were under pressure as well with the chasing pack of six clubs within four points in what was proving a highly-competitive campaign.

Having only managed to draw their previous home game 0–0 against third-placed West Brom, nothing less than a win would satisfy the capacity home crowd, with just over 2,000 travelling Burnley fans eager for their team to avenge a 4–2 home defeat by City earlier in the campaign – their only defeat at Turf Moor so far. Kevin Keegan demanded only one thing of his team – go out and attack and with the talismanic talents of Ali Benarbia and Eyal Berkovic scheming behind strikers Shaun Goater and Paulo Wanchope, he knew his instructions would be carried out to the letter. The 'Goat', with twenty-two goals under his belt already, was going through something of a lean patch by his standards and was goalless in the past four games, while his strike partner Wanchope hadn't scored for three months, though a knee injury accounted for most of that time. Stuart Pearce was still missing through injury and Shaun Wright-Phillips was on the bench, otherwise City were at full strength.

The Blues tore into Burnley straight from the kick-off and with just two minutes gone, Goater found space and crossed a low ball into the six-yard box where Wanchope slid the ball past Nick Michopoulos and into the net.

Gerard Wiekens picked up an injury on 21 minutes and was replaced by Richard Dunne, but the visitors were not leading the table by luck. They came into the game having won six out of their last seven matches and were unbeaten in their last ten. Their neat interplay saw them have plenty of possession without ever really threatening Carlo Nash's goal – until a controversial penalty was awarded for the Clarets midway through the half. Glenn Little stepped up only to see his shot saved by Nash

Danny Tiatto played his part in the Blues' surge towards the Premier League in 2001/2.

and not long after, Wanchope raced clear thanks to a sublime Benarbia through-ball and finished clinically with a low drive past Michopoulos to make it 2–0. Some of the Blues' passing was a joy to watch and as the home fans taunted the away section banked to the right of the North Stand, City went 3–0 up.

This time Wanchope and Goater combined superbly to lay off a chance for Berkovic on the edge of the box and the Israeli cracked home a fantastic shot to ensure the points were City's, even with almost an hour still to play. However, there was still more to come.

Berkovic and Benarbia were at their brilliant best with the Clarets simply being outclassed and on 44 minutes, City sent out a message that would send a shudder down the rest of the division's spine. Berkovic again slipped the ball perfectly through to Wanchope and the Costa Rican, in a carbon-copy of his second goal, calmly slipped the ball past Michopoulos to make it 4–0 at the break.

Maine Road stood as one to applaud the team off the field while Burnley's fans must have feared a cricket score. As so often happens though, the second half was something of an anti-climax, with the visitors settling for damage-limitation and the Blues playing pretty patterns but relaxed in the knowledge the job was as good as done. Ian Moore reminded the Blues they couldn't take their foot too far off the gas with a goal on 60 minutes to make it 4–1, but it was substitute Darren Huckerby who had the last word, running on to Berkovic's sublime pass to finish clinically and complete an impressive 5–1 victory.

A 3–1 win at Sheffield United three days later put City top while Burnley's confidence was shattered and they would win just one of their next seven League games and just two of their next eleven. The Blues romped to the title but Burnley didn't even make the play-offs, finishing seventh.

43 Mission Impossible

City 2, Gillingham 2 (City win 3–1 on pens)
Date: 30 May 1999
Competition: Division Two Play-Off Final
City: Weaver, Crooks (G. Taylor 85), Edghill, Wiekens, Morrison (Bishop 61), Horlock, Brown (Vaughan 61), Whitley, Cooke, Dickov, Goater
Attendance: 76,935

Where was the author? Slumped on my seat behind the goal without the energy to leave the stadium when we were 2–0 down.

It was in May 1999 when, arguably, City's renaissance really began. The Blues had endured a nervy, unimpressive first campaign in the nation's third tier and for long periods it seemed as though Joe Royle's side were destined to spend another season down among the dead men, and who knows what implications that may have had on the club's future?

A late burst for the play-offs started around the turn of the year and the Blues sustained enough form to finish in the top six, pitting them against Wigan Athletic for the right to face the winners of Preston North End and Gillingham at Wembley Stadium.

City drew the first leg against the Latics 1–1 at Springfield Park and won the second leg 1–0 courtesy of a Shaun Goater goal, while Gillingham surprisingly saw off much-fancied Preston North End over two legs to set up a showdown in the capital. There was a frenzy for tickets at both clubs, with the Blues asking for 50,000 and Gillingham 40,000. Wembley only held 80,000, but City argued that their average crowd was 30,000 compared with Gillingham's 8,000 or so, but the FA decided that the share should be equal, causing a great deal of discontent.

Ultimately, City were given around 40,000 tickets and Gillingham only slightly less and a record crowd for a Division Two play-off final was guaranteed. The Blues were the bookies' favourites to triumph, particularly as they'd appeared eleven times in various Wembley finals whereas this was the Gills' inaugural appearance at the Twin Towers.

City had injury concerns over skipper Andy Morrison and Ian Bishop, but both men were named in the squad with Mozzer starting and Bishop on the bench. The latter's exclusion from the starting line-up caused much chagrin among the Blues' followers who felt the classy midfielder could make the difference on Wembley's wide-open spaces – only time would tell.

From early in the game it was clear that Gillingham were in the final on merit and that this was going to be a close match. Plus Gills' 'keeper Vince Bartram – Paul Dickov's close friend – was in inspired form. The longer the game went on, the more nervy the City fans became, fearing one goal might be enough to settle the game either way, though as ever, expecting the worst. The limping Morrison was withdrawn and replaced by Tony Vaughan just past the hour and Michael Brown gave way to Bishop at the same time. Immediately City looked more cohesive as Bishop sprayed balls around the park in imperious fashion. With extra time looking likely, disaster struck when Carl Asaba burst through the City defence to toe-poke the ball into the roof of the net for Gillingham on 81 minutes. The City players and supporters were crestfallen and it was going to take a monumental effort to claw their way back into the game. Paul Dickov saw a point-blank shot saved by Bartram as the Blues chased an equaliser, but spaces appeared at the back and five minutes later Asaba back-heeled Robert Taylor through on goal and the Gillingham striker made it 2–0. 'Bye, bye Division Two!' crowed commentator Alan Brazil, 'It's party time in Kent tonight!' Who could blame him?

By the time the teams kicked off, there was 87 minutes on the clock and it looked as though it was game, set and match to Tony Pulis' side, but two minutes later, with thousands of City fans on their way out of Wembley, Kevin Horlock pulled one back with a low drive but to many, it was little more than scant consolation.

Then the board for added time went up and referee Mark Halsey indicated five extra minutes. Suddenly there was belief and still enough time to save the game – or was there? As the minutes ticked agonisingly by, the ball was launched upfield by Wiekens, nodded on by third sub Gareth Taylor towards Goater. The Goat's shot was charged down and the ball fell to Dickov 15 yards out. With 95 minutes played, this was it, the last-chance saloon – seconds later one end of Wembley went bananas as Dickov lashed the ball into the roof of the net.

Extra time brought close calls at either end, but it seemed a penalty shoot-out was going to be the only way to separate the two sides. City went first through Horlock who drilled the ball home for 1–0. Nicky Weaver then saved Gillingham's first effort but hero Dickov saw his spot-kick hit one post, then the other before rebounding out. Incredibly, Gillingham missed their next penalty, too, with Weaver not even required to make a save as the ball sailed past the post. Terry Cooke tucked his spot-kick past Bartram to make it 2–0 before the Gills finally found the back of the net. Richard Edghill cracked his kick in off the underside of the bar meaning if Gillingham missed their fourth penalty, City were up – and they did, as Weaver saved his second penalty of the shoot-out before setting off on a celebratory run that has become part of City folklore.

It doesn't matter that this game was a Division Two play-off final. It doesn't matter that the team the Blues beat was Gillingham and not Real Madrid – this was, quite simply, one of the most exciting games in the club's history and a day those who witnessed it will never forget.

City players celebrate their dramatic penalty shoot-out victory over Gillingham in the 1999 Division Two play-off final.

44 Marsh Class

CITY 2, BURNLEY 0
DATE: 22 DECEMBER 1973
COMPETITION: DIVISION ONE
CITY: MACRAE, PARDOE, DONACHIE, DOYLE, BOOTH, TOWERS,
SUMMERBEE, BELL, MARSH, LEE, LEMAN
ATTENDANCE: 28,114

Where was the author? Outside starting to kick a ball around in the street.

A distinctly average season threatened to get worse after an alarming autumnal dip in form by Ron Saunders' team saw the Blues slip from sixth place to fourteenth by mid-December. With just three wins in fourteen and a worrying lack of goals, matters were slightly improved by an impressive 2–0 win at Tottenham the week before third-placed Burnley were due at Maine Road.

Denis Law was unfit for the visit of the Clarets, but Franny Lee was back in after missing the Spurs match as City chased a sixth win in nine home games. The Blues had all the incentive they needed to beat Burnley having already lost 1–0 at home back in August in the FA Charity Shield. Worse still, City had also been comprehensively beaten 3–0 at Turf Moor by Jimmy Adamson's newly promoted side. During that game, Joe Corrigan was at fault for a couple of goals and after the game lost his place to Keith MacRae, a £200,000 signing from Motherwell.

The Maine Road pitch had cut up quite badly by late December and a crowd of just over 28,000 shivered in the winter sunshine. The Blues had reached the quarter-finals of the League Cup and came into the game having drawn 2–2 at Coventry City three days before so the promise of silverware kept the campaign ticking along, but the need to win the last match before Christmas was evident in the tense opening exchanges between the sides.

If anything, Burnley's football looked more coherent with several neat passing moves threatening early on and MacRae made a brilliant save to keep the score at 0–0. However, it was the Blues who broke the deadlock thanks to some shoddy defending from the visitors. The ball found its way out to Rodney Marsh on the left and the elegant forward seemed to have overrun the ball as the full-back approached. However, the hapless Claret stumbled and Marsh was able to take the ball back and cross to the back post where Colin Bell headed home.

Little else of note happened before the break and City came out for the second-half looking for a killer second, but again, James and Dobson drove Burnley forward in search of an equaliser only to be continually repelled by Mike Doyle and Tommy Booth. Lee tried to dance down the wing before being fouled and moments later Dobson clattered him again resulting in Lee attempting to take matters in his own hands as he aimed a kick at the Burnley man, fortunately missing his quarry, though he was clearly wound-up by what appeared to be a deliberate attempt to induce a reaction.

The best move of the game came when Willie Donachie won the ball on the left, played a one-two with Lee and then moved into the Clarets' half. As the young Scot fed Marsh, the main problem of the Blues' once rapier-like counter-attack became clear as Marsh trapped the ball, waited several seconds before switching play to the other flank. An exasperated Lee waved his arms in despair as the opportunity dissipated and the accusations that Marsh's style just didn't fit into this team garnered yet more weight.

City needed a second goal to settle the crowd down and midway through the second period, they got it. Mike Summerbee had been having one of his quieter games, but it was his left-wing corner that was met full on by Doyle whose header thundered in off the crossbar to make it 2–0. It was no more than Saunders' side deserved and but for an outrageous decision by the linesman, the score should have been 3–0 after Lee ghosted in at the back post to toe-poke the ball past Stevenson late on – TV replays proved he was a good yard on-side, but the goal was scrubbed off.

City's patchy season would see them finish in fourteenth – their lowest since 1967 – as well as lose the League Cup Final to Wolves. Saunders had proved an unpopular player in the dressing room and paid the ultimate price before the campaign had ended with the sack while Burnley went on to finish a highly creditable fifth in the table.

45   Charity Case

CITY 6, WEST BROMWICH ALBION 1
DATE: 3 AUGUST 1968
COMPETITION: CHARITY SHIELD
CITY: MULHEARN, CONNOR, PARDOE, DOYLE, HESLOP, OAKES, LEE,
BELL, SUMMERBEE, OWEN, YOUNG
ATTENDANCE: 35,510

Where was the author? Still chewing on a rusk.

Back in the days when charity began at home – literally – reigning league champions City took on FA Cup holders West Bromwich Albion in the annual top-flight curtain-raiser. It was the Blues' fourth Charity Shield match having lost 4–0 against Arsenal in 1934, beaten Sunderland 2–0 in 1937 and lost 1–0 to Manchester United in 1956. Having won the title on the final day of the 1967/8 season, the Blues had embarked on a mammoth month-long tour of the USA and the exhausted squad managed just one win in nine games against teams they would have normally been expected to beat with ease.

The Charity Shield venue was generally the home ground of the league champions with the first Wembley final still seven years away and sprinkled among the City fans were Albion supporters and even a Liverpool flag was spotted on the Kippax. With fully recharged batteries, Joe Mercer's side, featuring new signing Bobby Owen, walked out to a sun-drenched Maine Road in front of a more than respectable 35,510 fans with something of a point to prove. Albion had beaten City twice in five days during their title season and had been the only team to record a league double over the Blues.

The home support was still in celebratory mood, fully expecting their team to challenge strongly for the title once again and with the prospect of a first foray into the European Cup to look forward to. The BBC were covering the game for their *Match of the Day* highlights show later that evening and the great Kenneth 'they think it's all over' Wolstenholme would be providing the commentary. What nobody expected, however, was West Brom to take the word 'charity' to heart with a series of comical defensive mistakes from start to finish.

With barely a minute on the clock, a youthful Asa Hartford, then sporting Albion colours, played a poor pass into the middle which Colin Bell easily intercepted and then quickly played a 40-yard ball into the path of Mike Summerbee on the right flank. Buzzer spotted Owen's intelligent run and played a superb cross into his path and the former

Bury striker deftly placed the ball past Osborne in the Baggies' goal to get his City career off to a flying start.

Bell was dominating the middle of the park and he sprayed the ball out to Summerbee whose tempting cross was nodded into his own goal by Lovett to put City 2–0 up, but it was the third goal that proved just how brilliant and influential Bell, Francis Lee and Summerbee were to this magnificent Mercer/Allison side. A free-kick on the edge of the box suggested Lee was shaping up to smash the ball goalwards – the crowd thought as much and the Albion defenders certainly were convinced, but Lee ran past the ball as Bell instead passed it to Summerbee on the penalty spot, Buzzer then played it to Lee who had continued his run and the Blues' no. 9 slotted the ball home to make it 3–0. It was so simple, yet brilliant and innovative. Albion pulled a goal back on the stroke of half time through Krzywicki who broke through and rounded Ken Mulhearn with aplomb to reduce the arrears and give the travelling fans something to cheer, though their joy was short-lived.

Merrick replaced the hapless Osborne in goal at the break but the new Albion 'keeper's first job was to pick the ball out of the net after he allowed Owen's tame shot to somehow emerge from under his dive and trickle over the line. Terrible defending not long afterwards meant Mike Doyle's hopeful punt into the box suddenly became a good scoring chance for Neil Young after Fraser completely missed his attempt at a headed clearance and Young made no mistake with a typical rocket shot past Merrick, who must have wished he'd stayed on the bench.

The sixth and final goal was again partly down to defending that Billy Smart's Circus would have been proud of. Alan Oakes fed Bell on the left and his looping cross found Summerbee who nodded down to Lee. Lee's shot was straight at Merrick who capped a woeful display as he crouched to collect the ball by allowing it to somehow evade his grasp and trickle home for number six. For Albion, the final whistle couldn't come quickly enough on a day nobody from the Black Country will want to remember. Incredibly, the Blues almost gave West Brom a repeat dose of medicine in the league meeting four months later, winning 5–1 at Maine Road, but by then an oddly out-of-sorts City had slipped to sixteenth in the table, some six wins and 13 points adrift of league-leaders Liverpool.

46 Champions!

Newcastle United 3, City 4
Date: 11 May 1968
Competition: Division One
City: Mulhearn, Book, Pardoe, Doyle, Heslop, Oakes, Lee, Bell, Summerbee, Young, Summerbee
Attendance: 46,300

Where was the author? No idea – too small!

City travelled to Tyneside accompanied by the best part of 20,000 supporters, needing a win to guarantee the First Division title for the first time in thirty-one years. A magnificent 3–1 victory at Spurs the week before had set up a nerve-wracking final day that would become a regular occurrence for the Blues in future years. Though Liverpool were mathematically still in with a chance of winning the championship, it was City's neighbours from Old Trafford who posed the biggest threat and, if the Blues lost at St James' Park and United beat Sunderland, it would be the red half of Manchester celebrating the title.

That City were in with a chance of winning the league at all was a fantastic achievement considering they were a second division outfit just two years earlier. Under the legendary management team of Joe Mercer and Malcolm Allison, however, City had become a team who played entertaining football with a winning mentality. There were no passengers in this side – they were winners from 1 to 11 and even the flair players were grafters with a streak of steel. Mercer and Allison were supremely confident of victory against Newcastle and told the players as much in the week leading up to the match. 'That's it lads – there's no way we can lose now,' Mercer told the players on the train back from Tottenham, but the City faithful, weaned on years of drama and let-downs, were not so sure and the events of 11 May 1968 would prove they'd been right to err on the side of caution.

The Magpies may have been going into this game low on confidence having lost 6–0 to Manchester United the Saturday before and having tasted victory just once in eleven games, but they were determined to spoil the party. Buoyed by a big crowd, Newcastle were quick to put pressure on City and Scott saw a drive rattle the crossbar after just three minutes. The same player went close again before the irrepressible Mike Summerbee showed him how it was done by putting the Blues 1–0 up. The hosts immediately looked to respond and stunned City by levelling through Pop Robson a minute later. Then Tony Book was forced to clear

The Holy Trinity – Bell, Lee and Summerbee – at the heart of City's 1967/8 title success.

the ball off the line from future team-mate Wyn Davies – it was backs to the wall stuff that must have had the home faithful wondering why their team hadn't played like that every week.

It seemed whatever City did, Newcastle matched, and when questions were asked, they had the answers – as proved again when Neil Young fired City ahead again only for Sinclair to level maters again before half time. With a half-time pep talk from two of the best man-managers in the business, the Blues came out looking to kill off Newcastle once and for all and they took just four minutes to regain the lead. Colin Bell's fierce drive was parried by McFaul and Young was on hand to slot home his twenty-first goal of a fantastic season.

The goal restored the visitors' focus and belief and there was to be no riposte from the Geordies this time and when Bell put Francis Lee through mid-way through the second half. The City striker chipped the ball past McFaul to make it 4–2 and spark scenes of delirium among the travelling support.

McNamee pulled one back on 86 minutes, but the Blues saw the game out and in doing so confirmed the league title was heading back to Maine Road, not Old Trafford, where, incidentally, the Reds had gone down 2–0. Even if the Blues had lost, they'd have won the title, but this performance proved they were worthy winners.

47   The Life of Brian

BLACKBURN ROVERS 2, CITY 3
DATE: 17 APRIL 1995
COMPETITION: PREMIER LEAGUE
CITY: COTON, FOSTER, CURLE, KERNAGHAN, EDGHILL, SUMMERBEE,
FLITCROFT, SIMPSON, WALSH, ROSLER, QUINN SUB: BEAGRIE
ATTENDANCE: 27,851

Where was the author? Watching on Sky Sports I'm afraid!

City went to Ewood Park hovering precariously above the relegation zone. In contrast, Rovers were heading for the title and were strong favourites to dispatch Brian Horton's side who were struggling to string a couple of decent results together following a lull since Christmas. The match, televised live on Friday night for Sky Sports' watching millions, came at a time when the Blues were like rabbits in car headlights whenever they played live on TV. In fact, there was an audible groan around Manchester when the match was selected for coverage, so bad was City's record on Sky.

Still, there was hope. The loan signing of the mercurial Maurizio Gaudino had been just the boost Horton's flagging troops had needed and the Italian-sounding German midfielder had scored the winning goal for the Blues against Liverpool in the previous game, but had picked up an injury that kept him out of this clash.

Rovers, with the 'SAS' Shearer and Sutton attack, were quick to exploit the Blues' defensive frailties and went ahead when Tony Coton made a mess of a Keith Curle back-pass. The City skipper was quick to make amends, however, and with the atmosphere electrically charged, referee Keith Cooper spotted a foul on Niall Quinn just six minutes later and pointed to the spot. Curle dispatched the penalty with his customary coolness and City were level.

The Blues began to dominate the game, but after a couple of chances went begging, Rovers regained the lead following Colin Hendry's close-range stab home following a Stuart Ripley corner. Horton's men had every right to be frustrated as the half-time whistle blew with Rovers' 2–1 lead unmerited.

Perhaps feeling justice wasn't being done, the Blues started the second half determined to prove that they were every inch as good as the champions-elect and when the excellent Nicky Summerbee saw his cross cleared by Hendry on 57 minutes, the Blues levelled the scores as Uwe Rosler curled the ball past Flowers from the edge of the box to make

Keith Curle slots home another successful penalty in the 3–2 win over champions-elect Blackburn Rovers in 1995.

it 2–2. The United supporters must have been loving it: lying six points adrift of Rovers, here were their deadliest rivals doing them a massive favour – but there was more to come.

Paul Walsh and Quinn went close to putting City ahead for the first time before a running feud between Walsh and Graham Le Saux threatened to get out of hand. Le Saux appeared to elbow Walsh and when City were awarded a free-kick on the edge of the Rovers box, Walsh exacted his revenge by punching Le Saux out of the view of the referee but in plain view of the Sky cameras.

No action was taken and when Summerbee's free-kick fizzed in at speed, Flowers could only parry the ball and Walsh beat Atkins to the ball to put City 3–2 up on the night.

The goal was enough to win the game and, later, Rovers boss Kenny Dalglish said, 'Where have City been all season when they can play like that?' Where indeed? For the record, City beat relegation comfortably in the end, but a last-day 3–2 home loss to QPR saw Horton fired as the Blues' manager. Blackburn, thankfully, went on to win the title by one point, so no major damage had been done, after all.

48 We're Back!

City 5, Charlton Athletic 1
Date: 11 May 1985
Competition: Division Two
City: Williams, Lomax, Power, May, Clements, Phillips, Simpson, McNab, Melrose, Tolmie, Kinsey
Attendance: 47,285

Where was the author? With my brother Rowan, squashed on the Kippax.

The scenario City found themselves in on the final day of the 1984/5 campaign meant that the masses of supporters making their way to Maine Road on a scorching hot May afternoon did so with a mixture of dread and excitement – such is the life of a City fan. The rollercoaster existence of the club meant that, like a trip on a ride you didn't really want to get on, once you were strapped in, you had to wait until it was all over to regain control.

The Blues, managed by Billy McNeill, needed a win and nothing less. Portsmouth, with an inferior goal difference but the same points, were waiting to take the final promotion place should City fail. The Blues needn't have put their fans through the grinder yet again, having had the chance to clinch promotion a few days earlier at Notts County on Bank Holiday Monday. That day, City had lost 3–2 and blown the chance of enjoying their final fixture of the season in the knowledge they were guaranteed top-flight football again the following season. With just two wins from ten, the Blues had timed their worst run of the campaign to perfection and anything but a win would almost certainly see Pompey's late surge result in promotion.

The Kippax was full to bursting and around Maine Road, fans sat in aisles with every seat taken and the official crowd figure over more than 47,000 seemed to be several thousand off the mark. The atmosphere was electric and the fans, many buoyed by an extra few pints in the pub, were already in party mood.

The Blues were without the first-choice central defensive pairing of Mick McCarthy and Nick Reid and had instead to go with Kenny Clements and Andy May – a somewhat makeshift pairing at best. At least Jim Melrose was fit and Jim Tolmie, ill all week running up to the match, was also named in the starting eleven. The Blues began nervously and Charlton should have gone ahead but for a fine clearance off the line from Geoff Lomax but after 10 minutes, City started to string a few passes together and in their first real attack, David Phillips tucked the ball past

David Phillips completes the 5–1 rout over Charlton Athletic to secure promotion in 1985.

Charlton's teenage stand-in 'keeper to send the home fans wild. Then, just five minutes later, Paul Power's searching corner found the head of Andy May whose header looped high before dropping into the net for 2–0 – surely even the Blues couldn't cock this one up?

Chances came and went and when the referee blew for half time, there was still an element of doubt among the home fans who knew if Charlton pulled one back, the nerves would probably shred and anything could happen. City desperately needed a third – and they didn't have to wait long to get it. In fact, within 15 minutes of second-half action, the Blues had lifted the roof off Maine Road with three goals to lead 5–0 and just an hour played.

Melrose's powerful header made it 3–0, then Paul Simpson's persistence a minute later saw him nip between a hesitant defender and goalie to make it 4–0 and the dependable Phillips drilled home the fifth not long after. The game was over, promotion was assured and there was still 30 minutes to play – it was unheard of!

Charlton pulled back a late consolation goal, but the party had already begun and when the final whistle went to confirm City were back among the nation's elite, the home supporters invaded the pitch to celebrate in style.

49   Outgunned

City 4, Arsenal 2
Date: 12 September 2009
Competition: Premier League
City: Given, Richards, Bridge, Lescott, Touré, De Jong, Barry, Ireland, Bellamy, Adebayor, Tevez
Attendance: 47,339

Where was the author? Colin Bell Stand – loving every minute!

This match had the lot – skill, passion, drama and controversy by the bucket-load. The media played their part both before and after and the result was an explosive encounter that fairly crackled along at a breathless pace from start to finish. The main focus of the game was Emmanuel Adebayor. The Togolese striker had joined the Blues for £25m in the summer but his departure from Arsenal had been acrimonious at best with the supporters giving the player abuse while he was still playing for the club for allegedly expressing a desire to play for AC Milan – though he was never quoted as saying so.

Such was the bitterness that both parties were at pains to say how happy they were to be apart in the build up, so the match itself was a powder keg, waiting for the fuse to be lit. City had made a fantastic start to the campaign and went into the game full of confidence and belief – they'd beaten Arsenal 3–0 in the same fixture the season before and the Gunners' star hadn't been shining quite as brightly in recent years. But as both sides passed the ball around crisply, the Blues seemed to be building up a head of steam and on 19 minutes, City went ahead when Gareth Barry's free-kick was headed towards goal by Micah Richards. The ball struck the post, rebounded against Manuel Almunia's head and into the back of the net. That was to be the only goal of the first half that the Blues ended very much in the ascendency.

However, it was a completely different Arsenal that emerged for the second half. The slick passing and movement the Gunners have become famous for over the past decade began to cause City real problems and after incessant pressure, Robin van Persie turned on the edge of the City box and drilled a low drive past Shay Given to level the scores. The visitors continued to pressurise the Blues and it seemed inevitable they would go on and take all three points, but the second didn't arrive and gradually the Blues hauled themselves back into the game with their own slick counter attacks, one of which resulted in a second home goal.

Richards won the ball on the right and drove on to the Arsenal penalty area before squaring the ball to Craig Bellamy who lashed the ball past Almunia to make it 2–1 on 74 minutes. Five minutes later, Shaun Wright-Phillips found space on the right and crossed to the far post where Adebayor headed powerfully past Almunia to make it 3–1. His subsequent celebration of running from one end of the pitch to the other in order to slide in front of the visiting fans, who had taunted him from the pre-match warm-up onwards, caused crowd problems in the Arsenal section. A couple of dozen supporters even tried to get on to the pitch to confront the City striker who many felt was justified in his reaction. The repercussions were widespread condemnation and a suspended ban to go with a three-match ban for appearing to catch the irritating Van Persie in the face, but the City fans didn't care and when Bellamy broke to put Wright-Phillips in to deftly chip over Almunia for number four, the game was as good as over.

Tomas Rosicky did pull a goal back on 87 minutes and had van Persie's shot gone in a couple of minutes after that instead of striking the post, the last few minutes could have been very hairy indeed – but they weren't and City thoroughly deserved their victory.

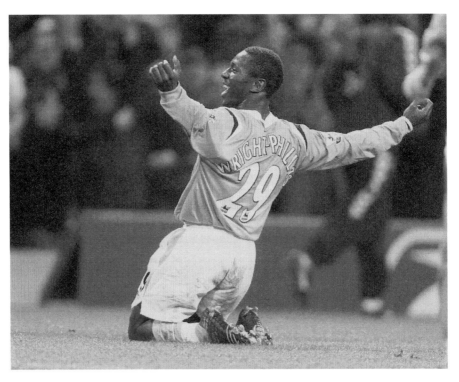

Shaun Wright-Phillips, on the mark during the 4–2 win over Arsenal in 2009.

50 Sheffield Steel

SHEFFIELD WEDNESDAY 2, CITY 6
DATE: 30 SEPTEMBER 2001
COMPETITION: DIVISION ONE (OLD)
CITY: WEAVER, PEARCE, GRANVILLE, EDGHILL (DUNNE), HOWEY,
TIATTO, WIEKENS, ETUHU (HORLOCK), BENARBIA, WANCHOPE, GOATER
(HUCKERBY)
ATTENDANCE: 25,731

Where was the author? Among the home fans keeping an (initially) low profile.

Ali Benarbia had barely begun his career with the Blues yet he already had the City fans eating out of his hand. It was unbelievable that such an incredible talent was not only without a club, but wouldn't cost a single penny in transfer fees. Now Kevin Keegan had a conductor to synchronise his orchestra and when Benarbia had the baton in his hand, the Blues played the sweetest music. The match against Sheffield Wednesday, probably more than any other, would show just what a genius the Algerian playmaker was.

It was to be an unforgettable day for the 6,000 or so Blues who made their way across the Pennines. With blue skies greeting the teams and an autumnal nip in the crisp air, the match soon burst into life when Wednesday's Pablo Bonvin bundled home after just two minutes to put the hosts 1–0 up with City not even in their stride. While the home fans taunted the packed away end, City gradually got into their stride and from a left-wing corner the ball fell to Benarbia who side-stepped two defenders before drilling a shot across Kevin Pressman and into the net for the equaliser.

City then went ahead five minutes later after Stuart Pearce's free-kick put Shaun Goater in sight of goal. The Goat still had plenty to do, but he held off Leigh Bromby's challenge to lob Pressman and put the Blues 2–1 up, a lead they held till the break, though the loss of Richard Edghill through a nasty knee injury just before half-time took the sheen off a decent display from Keegan's men.

Richard Dunne replaced Edghill but within 60 seconds of the restart, Wednesday were level following Bromby's thumping header. City, despite the blow, continued to play their expansive attacking game and were rewarded on 58 minutes when Goater chested down Benarbia's exquisite chip into the path of Danny Granville who tucked the ball away with aplomb.

City were by now in total control and gradually Wednesday began to fall apart. The Blues had to wait just nine more minutes to increase their lead to 4–2 and, once again, it was Benarbia at the centre of the move. The Algerian spotted Paulo Wanchope in acres of space and his sumptuous chip left the Costa Rican with a simple opportunity that he took. Benarbia then played in Goater with a slide-rule pass of such accuracy, it had to be seen to be believed. Goater made no mistake from a narrow angle to put his side 5–2 up, but the scoring still wasn't finished.

As the Owls fans drifted out in their thousands, substitute Darren Huckerby raced into the Wednesday box only to be hauled down by Danny Maddix. Wanchope stepped up to stroke the ball home and complete the scoring with still 12 minutes to play. Benarbia's virtuoso performances would win him the supporters' Player of the Year award as the Blues won promotion in a canter, playing a brand of football not seen at Maine Road in decades.

Gerard Wiekens, a solid, dependable utility player who became a huge crowd favourite during his time at Maine Road.

Top 20 Unforgettable FA Cup Moments

Here are twenty of the most memorable moments from 117 years of action in the world's most famous knockout competition

Liverpool Stanley? Who Are They?

In 1890 Ardwick FC took on Liverpool Stanley in the first-ever FA Cup tie. It was played in the first qualifying round at Hyde Road and was watched by a crowd of approximately 4,000. This wasn't, however, a precursor to the Manchester City v Liverpool clashes of the future as the Merseysiders weren't formed until 1892. Goals from Weir (3) and a couple each for Hidgetts, McWhinnie, Campbell and Rushton, plus one for Whittle completed the 10–0 rout. Ardwick then drew Halliwell away in the next round but the record books claim that Ardwick were 'scratched' and the first proper Round 1 tie wasn't until 1897 when the recently formed Manchester City lost 6–0 to the mighty Preston North End.

Bond Quits

If the FA Cup made John Bond's name with City, it arguably broke him as well. The maverick sheepskin-wearing, cigar-smoking manager had arrived in October 1980 and transformed an ailing City team into a slick, tough-to-beat outfit that became the cup team of the 1980/1 season. The Blues reached the 1981 FA Cup Final and should have won it, but for a large slice of rotten luck, and Bond was forever chasing that same successful high for the remainder of his City career. After dispatching Cardiff in the third round of the 1981/2 competition, the Blues slumped to a shock 3–1 home defeat to Coventry. The following season saw Bond's side hold Sunderland 0–0 at Roker Park and then beat them 2–1 at Maine Road, but the draw wasn't kind and Round 4 paired City with Brighton away. The Seagulls soared, won 4–0 and Bond walked. He'd had enough and his magic touch had deserted him.

'This Game Will Not Be Abandoned!'

City's 1976/7 FA Cup run was ended at Elland Road with hopes high of a trip to Wembley. Tony Book's side were going well in the league but faced their third successive tough draw after beating West Brom at The Hawthorns and Newcastle at St James' Park. Leeds away was one trip too many and City lost

1–0 in front of 47,731 fans. The following season, having missed out on the title by a single point to Liverpool, City were again drawn away to Leeds, this time in the third round. This time, the Blues raced into a 2–0 lead, courtesy of goals from Peter Barnes and Dennis Tueart and with around 10 minutes left, the Leeds fans swarmed on to the pitch in menacing fashion. The teams were hurriedly taken off and the home support obviously believed they could get the match abandoned and replayed but the referee announced there was no way this would happen and it was announced as much over the PA system. The game resumed and Leeds pulled one back, but City clung on for a famous win.

Sam Cowan's Promise

City were the cup kings of the early 1930s. Led by the superb Sam Cowan, City reached the semi-final in 1931/2, going down 1–0 to Arsenal at Villa Park, but a year later they went one better, and after taking an estimated 40,000 fans to Leeds Road, Huddersfield, for the 1932/3 semi-final, they dispatched Derby County 3–2 to make their first Wembley final for seven years to face Everton and the irrepressible Dixie Dean. Alas, it wasn't to be City's day and the men from Goodison Park triumphed 3–0. Choking back the tears, skipper Sam Cowan collected his loser's medal from King George VI who told Sam 'You played well.'

Sam managed to pull himself together and looked the king in the eye and said 'Thank you, sir, but we'll be back next year and win it.' The monarch was suitably impressed by Sam's remarks and watched him for a moment as he descended the steps. Sam would keep his word.

'Put Me On Now – I'll Get You A Goal, Boss.'

Clive Allen had achieved the status of cult hero at Manchester City but the one man he wasn't impressing also held the key to his future at the club. Peter Reid's preferred strike force was that of David White and Niall Quinn and Allen was reduced to climbing off the bench on occasion as his frustration grew to epic proportions. His 11 appearances during the 1990/1 season had all been as a sub and as City struggled to overcome Port Vale in the FA Cup fourth round, Allen was again sat in the dugout. With the scores level at 1–1, City won a corner with a few minutes remaining. Allen turned to Reid and promised him if he put him on for the corner, he'd grab a goal. The City player-boss, desperate to avoid a replay, agreed and managed to halt play in time for the change in personnel. Allen sprinted into the box, his shoelaces still not properly tied, took up his position and the ball duly found its way to him and he planted a winner into the back of the net. Simple game, football.

Biggest Provincial Crowd

Long before Manchester United tried to build stands that you needed a pilot's licence to sit in, the Blues were packing out Maine Road on a regular basis throughout 1934 with mammoth crowds, particularly in the FA Cup. More than 172,000 had seen the Blues over three home cup clashes but the best was yet to come as City drew Stoke in the quarter-final. Sam Cowan's men were on a mission and believed the FA Cup was their destiny and the fans were tapping into the dream. A record provincial crowd of 84,569 packed into Maine Road like sardines to witness Eric Brook score the only goal of the game and send City into the semi-finals. The record has lasted seventy-three years and despite United's endless building programme, it is the Blues that still hold the record to this day.

Crutches Away!

When it comes down to plain old raw passion, few goals have been celebrated quite ecstatically as the one during a third-round tie at Huddersfield Town in 1988. This was a special cup tie for many reasons, but the main one was the fact City had beaten the Terriers 10–1 in the league just eight weeks earlier. The hosts and their supporters saw this as an ideal opportunity for revenge but the Blues, backed by around 7,000 travelling fans, were in no mood for charity. Ian Brightwell put City 1–0 up after five minutes and that's how the score stayed until the break. Huddersfield came out in the second half like scalded cats and in the space of five minutes, had gone 2–1 up – and didn't their fans love it! This was payback time and the Blues' support had to grin and bear it. With 90 minutes up and no boards to indicate how long was left, it looked as though City were out, but the game just kept on going and with an incredible seven minutes of injury time played, City won a free-kick on the edge of Huddersfield's box. It was the very last chance and everyone knew it. John Gidman stepped up, curled the ball around the wall and into the back of the net. The City fans went wild and danced around Leeds Road's wide terraces for several minutes. One Blue who had hobbled in on crutches launched them into the air as he danced around – it truly was a miracle.

'And Rosler's Through On Goal.'

City were on something of a roll. Two defeats in ten games was quite a turnaround for a side that had failed to win any of their opening eleven Premiership matches and the FA Cup was something of a welcome distraction. Leicester City had been dispatched 5–0 after a third-round replay – a game that included a Kinkladze special. City then drew 2–2 with Coventry at Highfield Road before despatching the other Sky Blues 2–1 in the replay. There was genuine belief that a draw away to United was achievable and, but for an outrageous refereeing decision, it probably would have ended as such, if not better. With the score locked at 0–0, Kinky fed Uwe Rosler a sublime through ball and the German striker sent a delightful chip over the advancing Peter Schmeichel to put the Blues 1–0 up. Then, moments before the break, United won a corner and as the ball came across referee Alan Wilkie blew for an infringement. Roy Keane complained loudly then applauded as he realised he'd given a penalty for an alleged foul by Michael Frontzeck on Eric Cantona. United won 2–1 – it was a joke.

Big Mal's Return

Irony has always played a big role at City and there have been countless events over the years that would fit nicely under that label. The FA Cup fourth round draw in 1981/2 threw up several such instances and one of them was to pit the new City manager (and saviour) John Bond against the prodigal son and the man who had controversially stripped the team of most of its international stars during an ill-fated second spell in charge, which ended just a few months before. Allison was at his confident, brash best and with a posse of photographers he walked out before the match to salute the Kippax who gave Big Mal a mixed reception. Bond watched it all from the background and let his team do the talking – City won 4–0. There'll always be a place for Malcolm Allison in City fans' hearts, but this was business.

Sod's Law

There are certain things that have happened to City down the years that have shaped the club's character and that of their supporters. Some things happen that you could only imagine happening to Manchester City FC – and this is probably the daddy of them all. Picture the scene – a rain-soaked Kenilworth Road and the Blues were on fire. The question was, would the clock tick quickly enough or would the weather come to Luton's rescue? With just 21 minutes to go, City led 6–2 and Denis Law had scored all six. It was an amazing individual feat and it was a portent of things to come for young Law but, agonisingly, the referee decided enough was enough and abandoned the game – incredible! For history alone, surely the ref might as well have let play continue, but he didn't and as a mud-caked Law traipsed back to the dressing room, the game was rescheduled for four days later. You can probably see this one coming . . . City lost 3–1. The scorer? Denis Law.

'Richards Has Done It!'

City's FA Cup dream appeared to be over against one of their lucky sides. Trailing to Milan Baros' effort, Stuart Pearce's side seemed to be having 'one of those nights' when nothing would go their way. So when the board went up for four minutes of injury time, hopes of salvation were slim. Then Lee Croft won a corner with 94 minutes on the clock – this had to be the last chance. Croft swung the ball in and David James, who'd joined the final sortie, leapt up, missed but behind him and leaping even higher was Micah Richards who powered a header past Thomas Sorensen and into the net for the most dramatic of equalisers. City won a replay, beat Villa before exiting stage left to West Ham.

The First Trophy

Manchester City (under their new name) were just ten years old when they very nearly pulled off a prestigious league and cup double. It was season 1903/4 and Tom Maley's talented side were on the crest of a wave having been crowned Division Two champions the season before. They were heading towards the league title and had reached the prestigious FA Cup Final for the first time where they would face Bolton Wanderers, not at Wembley, rather 'The Crystal Palace', London. More than 61,000 fans turned London into a little piece of Lancashire for the day but it was the City fans who travelled home with beaming smiles after Billy Meredith's controversial goal won the game (Bolton claimed he was offside). Sheffield Wednesday just pipped City for the league to spoil an otherwise memorable campaign.

Record Semi-Final Win

The Blues were breaking records left, right and centre. The goals were flying in, the fans were flocking to watch and the team were on a mission to bring the FA Cup home to Manchester for only the second time. It was back to Leeds Road, Huddersfield, for the semi-final where City would face Aston Villa, a team they'd already had two tight matches with in the league – 0–0 and a 1–0 win in City's favour. Aiming to fulfil Sam Cowan's prophecy of returning to Wembley to win after being losing finalists the year before, City set about Villa like a pack of hyenas on a stricken beast. Fred Tilson helped himself to four goals while Alec Herd and Ernie Toseland grabbed one each in a breathtaking 6–1 victory that is still the biggest winning margin in an FA Cup semi-final to this day.

Hutch's Header

Tommy Hutchison was a genius and a delight to watch. Part of the fabled Tartan Trio that helped transform a sorry City team into a slick, solid side that specialised in cup-ties, he was sadly at the wrong end of what should have been a glittering career. His silky skills, vision and trickery made him an instant favourite with the City fans and it was perhaps fitting that he should score City's opening goal of the 1981 FA Cup Final. As the Blues pressed for an opener, the ball found its way to Ray Ranson, who whipped in a perfect ball that Hutchison launched himself at, connected sweetly with and headed home to put his side 1–0 up. It looked for so long as though that would be enough, but in a cruel twist of fate, well, you know the rest and the game ended 1–1 with the name of Tommy Hutchison credited with a goal for each team.

Freddy's Revenge

Fred Tilson was one of City's greatest strikers and he was a constant irritation in opposition penalty boxes throughout the early 1930s. He forged a terrific partnership with prolific Eric Brook but was left heartbroken when, despite being given a certificate of fitness for the 1933 FA Cup Final, the medical staff was still concerned that his injury problem might force him to break down and he was left out of the team that lost 3–0 to Everton. The team were determined to return and win the following year and spearheading the charge was Tilson who scored seven goals as the Blues marched to their second consecutive final. This time, Tilson was injury-free and he inspired his team-mates to victory with two goals in a 2–1 win over Portsmouth.

Power Aid

City had made their second semi-final of the season having reached the same stage in the League Cup. They faced Ipswich for the honour of competing in the Centenary FA Cup Final of 1981 but began as outsiders against Bobby Robson's slick high flyers. Villa Park was the destination and the Blues' lucky ground didn't disappoint. Many felt the final was City's destiny, but fans of most clubs generally do when they reach the last four of any competition. Ipswich came close on several occasions but City held out to force extra time. In one of those ironic moments mentioned earlier, the Blues were awarded a free-kick just outside the Ipswich box. Paul Power stepped up to curl a magnificent shot into the top corner to send half of Villa Park crazy. The timing of the goal? The 100th minute of the 100th FA Cup competition.

Mackenzie!

This was a goal that has largely been forgotten over the years, mainly thanks to the goal that was scored by Ricky Villa later in the same game. Nobody can take away the fact that City's teenage midfielder volleyed home one of the best goals ever seen at Wembley, however, and it's certainly one he can replay over and over with his grandchildren in years to come. The big question is, was Villa's goal really better? It was the winner, sure, but when you dissect the Argentine's run and toe-poke, great goal though it was, it wasn't as technically good as Mackenzie's. City had gone down to an early Steve Archibald goal when the ball fell to Tommy Hutchison. Hutch cushioned a header perfectly into Mackenzie's path and he cracked home a perfect volley from just outside the box. It deserved a better fate than being consigned to the 'losers' goals archive.

Young at Heart

There seems to be something of a curse – or at least there was – on players who scored winning FA Cup Final goals and though Neil Young's post-cup final career certainly doesn't fit into that category, within a couple of years he was struggling to find the form that had made him such an integral part of the Mercer-Allison glory days. If there is a price to pay for such a glorious epitaph, some would say it's well worth it. Young scored the only goal of the 1969 cup final, after great work by Mike Summerbee and his searing left-foot drive from near the penalty spot was worthy of winning any final.

Mission Possible

It would take a special occasion to pip three cup final victories and a couple of memorable semi-finals but City's incredible comeback against Spurs in 2004, was arguably one of the club's greatest ever games. In case there are a few of you out there unfamiliar with the scenario, Kevin Keegan's side went 3–0 down just before the break, had lost Nicolas Anelka to injury and then had Joey Barton sent off after the whistle for half time. It was damage limitation and nothing more – or at least, that's what everyone thought. If the impossible was to happen, a very strict set of events would have to ensue. One: early goal back – check. Two: second goal midway through the second half – check. Three: equaliser before last 10 minutes – check. Four: don't allow extra time and score with virtually the last act of the game – check. That's all how it panned out and Jon Macken's perfect header sealed a fantastic night to be a City fan and a 4–3 win against all odds.

Braveheart

Any which way you look at City's most incredible moments in the FA Cup, nothing – nothing at all – comes even close to the act of bravery shown by Bert Trautmann in the 1956 FA Cup Final. City had led through Joe Hayes' 3rd-minute goal, but Birmingham equalised on 15 minutes. Jack Dyson restored the maroon and white-striped Blues (stay with me) in the second half and two minutes later, Bobby Johnstone made it 3–1. Having endured the pain of defeat a year earlier at the hands of Newcastle, City were in no mood to let this chance slip through their fingers but with 75 minutes on the clock, Bert Trautmann dived at Birmingham striker Murphy's feet and his knee followed through into the German 'keeper's neck. Think Petr Cech and Stephen Hunt of Reading times two. There were no subs allowed back then and the thought of City putting an outfield player in goal just wasn't considered as Trautmann made it clear he would play on. Despite the excruciating pain, he saw the game through to the end without conceding a goal before being helped from the pitch a hero. Later diagnosed with a broken neck, one more knock could have seen him spend the rest of his days in a wheelchair and he spent the next seven months recovering. An unforgettable, selfless performance from a truly great man.

Top 20 League Cup Ties

It's 34 years since the Blues last tasted success in the League Cup – here are the twenty best matches the club have been involved with since the competition began in 1960.

City 3, Stockport County 0
Round 2, 18 October 1960

City's first venture into the League Cup began in the autumn of 1960 with a local derby against Stockport County. With such luminaries as Bert Trautmann, Joe Hayes, Denis Law and Ken Barnes playing for the Blues, a crowd of 21,065 – about 10,000 below average – watched Law score twice (his sixth and seventh strikes of the season) and Hayes add another in a comprehensive victory. City again drew lower league opposition in Round 3 but lost 2–0 at Portsmouth.

City 2, Sheffield Wednesday 1
Round 2, 2nd leg, 4 September 1979

Having drawn 1–1 in the first leg at Hillsborough, the Blues took on the Second-Division Owls at Maine Road in front of a crowd of 24,000. Wednesday took the lead late on in controversial circumstances when Joe Corrigan saved a spot-kick only for it to be ordered to be retaken. This time Joe was beaten and Wednesday appeared to be edging Malcolm Allison's struggling side out of the competition. But two dramatic goals from midfielder Tony Henry in the last two minutes sent the City fans wild and it was the hosts who progressed into the third round.

Liverpool 1, City 1
Semi-Final, 2nd leg, 10 February 1981

City travelled to Anfield trailing 1–0 from the first leg and still feeling a sense of injustice following Kevin Reeves' seemingly perfectly legal goal being ruled out at Maine Road. Pumped up and desperate to cause an upset, the Blues turned on the style and despite falling behind, continued to press forward, finally being rewarded with a Reeves equaliser. Not used to being pressed on their own patch, Liverpool looked edgy and when Dave Bennett crashed a header onto the bar, the Blues' best chance came and went and they valiantly bowed out 2–1 on aggregate to the Merseysiders.

Stoke City 2, City 0
Round 2, 2nd leg, 28 October 1981

Not an obvious choice for a favourite tie, perhaps, but a game full of drama, tension and ultimately celebration for the Blues. This was the second year in succession that City and Stoke had faced each other in the second round over two legs. Asa Hartford and an own goal gave John Bond's side the advantage as the second leg began. Stoke were up for the battle this time, and levelled the aggregate twice during the 90 minutes' action, though nobody scored in extra time. A penalty-shoot out ensued with both teams converting eight each before Corrigan saved. It was left to Aage Hariede to score from the spot and give City a 9–8 win – still the highest total the club have been involved in.

City 5, Notts County 1
Round 4, 29 October 1980

If City ever had one player they could label a 'talisman' for the League Cup, it is undoubtedly Dennis Tueart who seemed to make a habit scoring in the competition with 18 goals in 27 appearances. For all the games and great goals he scored, he never bettered his haul on this evening against Jimmy Sirrell's hapless side – always good fodder for the Blues in this cup. Tueart set about a one-man destruction of County with a virtuoso display that was head and shoulders above anybody else. His four goals – plus one from Dave Bennett – gave City a 5–1 win and a place in the last eight – a win that was curiously mirrored some fifteen years later in the FA Cup when the Blues beat the same opposition 5–2 with Uwe Rosler scoring four times.

City 3, Nottingham Forest 0
Round 3, 27 October 1987

There wasn't much to smile about in the dim mid-1980s gloom that seemed to permanently hover over Maine Road. Gates were down and there was no money in the kitty for boss Mel Machin so the visit of top-flight Nottingham Forest for a place in the last sixteen wasn't greeted with that much enthusiasm by the 15,168 fans that turned up on a chilly October evening. However, Machin's side was beginning to click and when they hit top gear, they were a force to be reckoned with. Forest skipper Stuart Pearce would not have been pleased with his side's display as Imre Varadi scored twice and Paul Stewart added a third to dump Brian Clough's team out.

Newcastle United 0, City 2
Round 4, 21 December 1994

In a season of dramatic ups and downs, City were at their unpredictable best as they travelled to St James' Park to try to earn a place in the quarter-finals for the first time since 1988. The two teams, both starved of silverware, had battled out a 1–1 draw at Maine Road and were equally desperate of progressing to a possible Wembley appearance. City had dished out several thrashings in the Premiership already, but had been well beaten on several occasions, too, so it was into the unknown on a bitter evening in the north-east. Fortunately, it was a 'can-do' performance, both gutsy and attacking and Rosler and Paul Walsh both scored to give City a 2–0 victory and send the travelling army home both delighted and a little shocked at a rare win in Newcastle.

Plymouth Argyle 3, City 6
Round 2, 2nd leg, 12 October 1988

Plymouth returned to the West Country content at the 1–0 deficit from the first leg clash at Maine Road. The Blues were battling away at the top of the table and scoring freely but the Pilgrims must have fancied their chances of turning the tie around. But on an evening of sheer entertainment at Home Park, the Blues plundered six of the nine goals scored that evening. Wayne Biggins, Paul Moulden, Nigel Gleghorn (2), Neil McNab and Paul Lake all scored making the midweek trek south-west well worthwhile for the 1,000 or so travelling Blues.

City 7, Notts County 1
Round 1, 2nd leg, 19 August 1998

With City still trying to come to terms with life in the nation's third tier, opening week wins over Blackpool and then Notts County in the League Cup were most welcome. A 3–0 reverse at Fulham, however, and the old doubts resurfaced and seeing Notts County off in the second leg became of paramount importance. The crowd of 10,063 may have been sparse, but those who turned up were glad they had as Joe Royle's men went to town on the Magpies, banging seven goals in with Jim Whitley and Gary Mason grabbing their first (and only) goals for City and Paul Dickov and Shaun Goater each scoring twice and Lee Bradbury also netting. It was a huge confidence-booster and the 9–1 aggregate win was in no way flattering.

City 6, Birmingham 0
Round 3, 10 October 2001

Birmingham had already been well-beaten 3–0 in the league by Kevin Keegan's exciting side when they were paired together for a repeat meeting just four weeks later. This was to be Darren Huckerby's evening and he proceeded to dismantle the visitors' defence with a mix of electric pace and clinical finishing and the tie was as good as over at the break with the Blues 3–0 to the good. It was more of the same in the second period and Huckerby finished with four and a Goater strike and an own goal left Steve Bruce's boys heading down the M6 with a 6–0 tanning.

City 7, Barnsley 1
Round 2, 21 September 2004

Barnsley brought a large and vociferous following to the City of Manchester Stadium to try to shout their team to a surprise win, but it was all in vain as the Blues turned on the style to go in 5–0 up at the break. Such was the canter that many wondered if double figures were on the cards, but the Tykes improved in the second half and lost the game 7–1. The pick of the goals was Joey Barton's 30-yard scorcher with Shaun Wright-Philips' delightful chip also worthy of mention. Jon Macken and Antoine Sibierski both scored a couple and Willo Flood also found the net on an easy evening's work for Keegan's side.

City 3, Liverpool 2
Round 3, 24 September 1969

It was City v Merseyside in the opening three rounds of the 1969/70 League Cup with City facing Southport, Liverpool and Everton. Incredibly, though this game took place in September, Liverpool had already completed a league double over Joe Mercer's side and the Blues knew that if they were to see off Bill Shankly's men, they'd have to do so at the first attempt. The crowd was below 30,000 but the tie was an epic cup tie and goals from Mike Doyle, Ian Bowyer and Neil Young gave City victory and a belief that would eventually see them lift the trophy six months later.

Norwich City 1, City 6
Round 2, 2nd replay, 24 September 1975

Back in the days when replays were needed to settle games, City and Norwich locked horns in the League Cup second round in a tie that would take three games to settle. The Blues were fortunate to leave Carrow Road with a 1–1 draw, initially, with Dave Watson's goal setting up a Maine

Road replay. Strikes from Royle and Tueart were not enough to see off John Bond's plucky outfit who again held solid to draw 2–2 in front of almost 30,000 fans. The third game had to be played at a neutral venue and Stamford Bridge – a sizeable distance from both clubs – was deemed the perfect venue. With only 6,238 hardy souls bothering to turn up, City took the Canaries to the cleaners with Tueart scoring a hat-trick and further goals from Royle and Mike Doyle, plus and own goal, completing a 6–1 rout.

QPR 3, City 4
Round 3, 25 October 1994

Brian Horton's attack-minded City travelled to Loftus Road for the second time in ten days in search of a place in the last sixteen. It was to be an epic encounter with goals and incidents galore as both sides went flat-out for victory but it was the red and black striped visitors who edged the seven-goal thriller. The pick of the goals was Nicky Summerbee's acrobatic volley that flew into the roof of the net, with Steve Lomas, Peter Beagrie and a Keith Curle penalty completing a 4–3 win.

City 4, Middlesbrough 0
Semi-Final, 2nd leg, 21 January 1976

City had to storm out of the blocks if they were to overturn Middlesbrough's controversial 1–0 first leg lead for a place in the 1976 League Cup Final – and that's exactly what they did. City were 2–0 up as early as 11 minutes into the match thanks to strikes from Alan Oakes and Ged Keegan and further goals from Peter Barnes and Joe Royle gave Tony Book's youngsters (seven were home-grown talents) a richly-deserved 4–0 win in front of 44,426 Maine Road fans. It also gave City their third final appearance in just six years at a time when the club were one of the most successful in the competition.

City 2, Manchester United 1
Semi-Final, 1st leg, 3 December 1969

This tie remains the closest City and United have ever got to contesting a major cup final. Many were disappointed when the old foes were paired together, but more so the Reds who rarely beat the Blues during the 1960s. City had beaten United 4–0 eighteen days earlier in the league derby and now they had to avoid another heavy loss to keep their hopes of reaching the final alive. With 55,799 crammed into Maine Road, it was City who edged a tight affair with goals from Bell and Lee and the return leg was equally fraught, with City withstanding United's assault to draw 2–2 and go to their first League Cup Final and the first of the new decade.

City 2, Plymouth Argyle 0
Semi-Final, 2nd leg, 30 January 1974

Second-Division Plymouth Argyle were the surprise package of the 1973/4 League Cup and many neutrals were willing them to beat City and reach the final once the draw had been made. A hard-fought first leg at a packed Home Park had ended 1–1 with Tommy Booth scoring for the Blues, now under the stewardship of Ron Saunders. More than 40,000 attended the midweek return leg and goals from Bell and Lee were enough to see off their plucky lower league opponents. City marched on to the final only to put on a below-par display and lose 2–1 to Wolves.

City 4, Manchester United 0
Round 4, 12 November 1975

An unforgettable clash of the Manchester giants for many reasons, but the injury to Colin Bell overshadowed all else on what should have been a joyous night for City fans. The newly promoted United had already secured a 2–2 draw at Maine Road six weeks earlier and arrived at Maine Road in confident mood for a place in the quarter-finals. But it was City who dominated and ran out emphatic winners with goals from Tueart (2), Royle and Hartford delighting the majority of the 50,182 crowd. Martin Buchan's challenge on Bell was effectively the beginning of the end for the City legend and even a 4–0 win over the old enemy couldn't erase the sad sight of the Blues greatest player being stretchered off with his career in tatters.

WBA 1, City 2
League Cup Final, 7 March 1970

Snow-covered Wembley and the churned-up mess beneath it led to Joe Mercer famously calling it a 'pig of a pitch'. The Horse of the Year Show had ensured a scrappy contest on a muddy surface that threatened to derail Mercer's slick passing City side. Indeed, West Brom's Jeff Astle opened the scoring on six minutes with a typically powerful header and a travel-weary City side (they'd just returned from Portugal in a European Cup Winners' Cup tie) looked as though they would struggle to recover. But this was a team of winners and on the hour, Doyle made it 1–1 to take the game into extra time where Glyn Pardoe emerged as the unlikely hero, scoring after 102 minutes to secure a first League Cup triumph for the Blues.

City 2, Newcastle United 1
League Cup Final, 28 February 1976

The 1976 League Cup Final will always hold a special place in most City fans' hearts and thanks to Dennis Tueart, it's also one of the best-remembered Wembley finals ever. With 100,000 fans crammed into the old stadium, Peter Barnes poked the Blues ahead only for the Geordies to equalise. With the game evenly poised, Tommy Booth headed a free-kick back across the face of the six-yard box where Tueart, with his back to goal, launched himself into a spectacular bicycle kick to win the game for City and deliver manager Tony Book's first piece of silverware. It is the last knock-out trophy the club won and that's a record nobody at the time could ever have envisaged – and one that Roberto Mancini will be keen to put right as soon as possible.

Top 20 European Nights

The Blues last tasted success in Europe forty years ago, but here are the twenty best ties to date.

Fenerbahçe 0–0
18 September 1968

City went into their first European match against Turkish champions Fenerbahçe in the midst of an awful run in the league which had seen them win just one of their opening nine games, leaving them teetering above the relegation zone. That, plus Malcolm Allison's pre-match claim that City would 'terrify Europe' seemed to affect the Blues and the naivety and inexperience showed in a tough first leg of a tie that the Turks would edge 2–1 in the second leg.

Linfield 1–1
16 September 1970

When City drew the Northern Irish part-timers Linfield in the first match since winning the European Cup Winners' Cup six months earlier, few looked upon the tie as anything but a comfortable journey into the second round. The reality, however, was a rather uncomfortable passage and the second leg saw the Blues visibly edgy being in a country experiencing horrific civil disturbances and there was even a point Linfield boss Billy Bingham was forced to walk in front of his own fans' Kop to plead with them to stop throwing missiles onto the pitch. Colin Bell's solitary effort at Maine Road was enough to give the Blues a slender lead to take across the water, but Linfield almost caused a huge upset by winning the second leg 2–1, almost grabbing a late third but Francis Lee's goal ultimately proved decisive as City scraped through on the away goals rule.

Lokeren 3–2
24 September 2003

Having qualified for the UEFA Cup for the first time in twenty-five years, the Blues had high hopes of progressing to the second round against a team that were considered as no more than an average, workmanlike outfit by most pundits. But backed by a 500 or so noisy travelling fans, the Belgians refused to buckle on the night and twice pegged City back in a five-goal thriller. Antoine Sibierski, Robbie Fowler and a penalty from Nicolas Anelka were enough to tilt the tie in the hosts' favour but 3–2 was a dangerous lead

FC Twente 3–2
27 September 1978

Having secured a 1–1 draw in Holland in the first leg, City began in confident mood against FC Twente and goals from Brian Kidd, Colin Bell – his first in Europe for eight years – and an own goal just saw off the plucky Dutch side who refused to throw the towel in, but ultimately bowed out 4–3 on aggregate.

TNS 5–0
14 August 2003

How do you follow a stadium-opener like Barcelona? Easy, by playing Welsh non-League side Total Network Solutions in a UEFA Cup qualifier, of course. With a gate of 34,103 filling the two tiers of the ground that were open, this was a game City couldn't really lose. They were expected to run up a cricket score and they went part-way with a 5–0 win. Trevor Sinclair scored the first official goal at the City of Manchester Stadium with a crisp 20-yard volley and Wright-Phillips, Sun Jihai, David Sommeil and Anelka scored the others.

Lokeren 1–0
15 October 2003

It had been a long time since the majority of City fans had last tasted football abroad so it was no surprise that almost half the 10,000 crowd at Lokeren's tiny Daknamstadion were from Manchester. The tie was delicately balanced and Lokeren clearly fancied their chances, safe in the knowledge that a 1–0 or 2–1 win would see them into the next round. As it was, the colourful autumnal evening was settled by an Anelka penalty and the majority of the Blue Army headed to Brussels airport hoping for more of the same.

SK Lierse 5–0
26 November 1969

The 5–0 win over Belgian side SK Lierse would remain the Blues' biggest win in European competition for thirty-four years – and has only been equalled in 2003. The match was over as a contest in the first leg when City won comfortably 3–0 with goals from Franny Lee (2) and Bell and it was the same pair that grabbed a couple each in the return at Maine Road with Mike Summerbee completing the rout. The 8–0 aggregate score remains the club's best to date.

Gornik Zabrze 2–0
24 March 1971

City were on the end of a 2–0 thrashing as the1970 European Cup Winners' Cup finalists again locked horns for the right to progress to the semi-finals for the second successive year. Goals from Ian Mellor and Mike Doyle meant the tie was level at 2–2 and with no penalties to settle the tie, a fourth meeting of the teams in eleven months was arranged for a neutral venue.

Valencia 2–2
13 September 1972

With twenty European ties in just four years, the Blues players and fans sorely missed playing against the cream of Europe in season 1971/2, so qualification for the 1972/3 UEFA Cup was welcomed and gave the supporters a chance to once again dust off their passports and travel to exotic locations to support their heroes. Trouble was, Valencia failed to capture the paying public's imagination and just 21,698 turned up at Maine Road for what was to be a cracking tie. Ian Mellor and Rodney Marsh scored City's goals but the Spaniards left with a creditable 2–2 draw and won the second leg 2–1 to dump the Blues out at the first hurdle.

Gornik Zabrze 3–1
31 March 1971

Copenhagen was deemed the perfect venue to decide the replayed third round ECWC tie between City and old foes Gornik and it was hardly surprising only 12,100 turned up to watch the match. The Blues didn't dally around in this match and, determined to defend their title, they brushed aside the Poles with goals from Tommy Booth, Lee and Neil Young securing a 3–1 win. Chelsea awaited in the semis but an injury-hit City lost both legs 1–0.

Borussia Mönchengladbach 1–1
7 March 1979

There were few teams more feared or respected throughout the 1970s than Borussia Mönchengladbach. City drew the Germans in the last eight of the UEFA Cup and it was the worst pairing possible for Tony Book's side, but they made a decent fight of it in front of almost 40,000 Maine Road fans. Channon's goal gave the Blues hope, but Borussia had too much in their locker and finished the job in the return leg by winning 3–1.

Atletico Bilbao 3–3
17 September 1969

Few performances on the continent could match the thrilling display City gave in Bilbao as they returned to European action after the disappointment of the Fenerbahce experience. Though they found themselves 2–0 down and 3–1 down, the Blues refused to buckle and two late goals ensured a 3–3 draw on the night and the teams returned to Manchester on level terms with City confident of progression to the next stage.

Academica Coimbra 1–0
18 March 1970

City had discovered that the Portuguese university side were a tough, uncompromising quarry in the quarter-final clash in Coimbra. Indeed Joe Mercer's side were relieved to head home with a hard-fought 0–0 draw under their belts. Having just won the League Cup, confidence was high of reaching the last four, but it proved another uncomfortable 90 minutes with still no goals scored. With the prospect of a replay looming, Tony Towers scrambled home a late winner in extra time to send Maine Road wild and book a place in the semi-finals.

Standard Liege 4–0
18 October 1978

Yet more Belgian opposition for City – this time in the form of a decent Standard Liege side. Things seemed to be going according to plan for the visitors when, with 85 minutes gone, they trailed just 1–0. The Blues, however, were far from finished and further goals from Brian Kidd (his second of the night), Roger Palmer and Asa Hartford made it three in five minutes and effectively ended Liege's hopes of progression, though they gallantly rallied to win the second leg 2–0.

AC Milan 2–2
23 November 1978

City almost wrote their name into the history books as they travelled to Italy to face perhaps their most illustrious opponents yet. AC Milan had never lost to English opposition and as the sides prepared for the match, the Italians, packed with seasoned internationals, were confident they could see off Book's men. But a thick fog descended causing the game to be abandoned and arranged for the following afternoon – unthinkable by today's standards. Bereft of the partisan atmosphere and firecrackers that charged Milan home ties with electricity, City raced into a shock 2–0 lead thanks to goals from Kidd and wonderful solo effort from Paul Power. The hosts hit back to draw 2–2 but City had struck a mighty blow and now found themselves as unlikely favourites to move into the last eight.

Atletico Bilbao 3–0
1 October 1969

Euro fever had captured the City fans' imagination with just shy of 50,000 fans cramming into Maine Road to see if their team could win their first European tie – and they weren't disappointed. Fresh from a 2–0 defeat at Stoke, the Blues gave a polished performance that oozed class and panache – too much for the Spaniards who had no reply to Ian Bowyer, Alan Oakes and Colin Bell's goals. This performance would give Mercer's side the confidence to power on in the competition and take on all-comers.

Juventus 1–0
15 September 1976

Few more talented sides have arrived at Maine Road for a competitive match than the star-studded Juventus team of season 1976/7. Containing half the Italian national team and with a defence that O.J. Simpson would have been proud to have in front of him, it was perhaps the toughest draw City could have had for their first UEFA Cup match. But with seven clean sheets from ten European matches, the Blues were formidable opposition on their own patch and backed by almost 37,000 fans, City played a cagey game and had clearly done homework on the Turin giants. Brian Kidd scored the only goal of the game but, despite a sterling effort, one goal always seemed a precarious lead to take to the Stadio Delle Alpi and so it proved as the Old Lady, in typical style, did just enough with a 2–0 win and went on to win the competition.

AC Milan 3–0
6 December 1978

A modern-day favourite for kids growing up in the 1970s (i.e. me) as the Blues levelled European giants AC Milan with perhaps the best first half ever seen at Maine Road. Just as had happened at the San Siro, City were out of the blocks like men possessed and Milan had no answer to the fast-paced attacks and goals from Kidd, Booth and Hartford sent the

Italians in reeling at the break. From there on, it was damage limitation as the visitors settled for defeat so long as no more goals were conceded. A memorable night.

Schalke 04 5–1
15 April 1970

While beating Milan remains a fantastic achievement, City's greatest European night at Maine Road was undoubtedly the semi-final second leg clash with crack German outfit Schalke 04. City had pegged their opponents back in the first leg and come away trailing by a single goal. Having still never conceded a goal at home in Europe, City were confident that they could progress to their first final in Europe at the only their second attempt. Pumped up and willed on by 46,361 fans, the Blues were irresistible and romped home thanks to goals from Neil Young (2), Bell, Lee and Mike Doyle and despite a late consolation ruining the clean sheets record, the 5–1 scoreline was celebrated long into the night by Blues fans who could look forward to a glamorous final and the prospect of yet more silverware to add to an already bulging trophy cabinet. It was exhilarating, heady stuff by arguably the best team in Europe at that point.

Gornik Zabrze 2–1
29 April 1970

The Blues' opponents were Polish outfit Gornik Zabrze – champions in their homeland eight times out of the previous twelve years, and who had among their number Eastern Bloc superstar Włodzimierz Lubański. The Poles had already seen off Olympiakos, Glasgow Rangers, Levski-Spartak and one of the tournament favourites, AS Roma, in the semis. But it was City who registered their intentions early on and the early pressure paid off when Young slotted home after 12 minutes. Young was again involved in City's second of the night on 43 minutes, winning a penalty which Franny Lee hammered home. Ozilzlo pulled one back on 68 minutes but the Blues held on to record a famous win.

And Here's 10 Games to Forget . . .

You can't have a sugary-sweet book without just a hint of a bitter aftertaste. It's character-building to take the rough with the smooth and, with that in mind, here are ten brief reminders of games that didn't quite go according to plan.

City 2, Widzew Łodz 2
UEFA Cup, 1977

City had been expected to progress in Europe having drawn little-known Polish side Widzew Łodz. After leading by two clear goals with nineteen minutes remaining, the Blues were pegged back by an inspirational and as yet more or less completely unknown Zbigniev Boniek, who, not content with scoring both the goals that drew his side level at Maine Road, then walked to the City fans arms outstretched in glee after netting his side's equaliser from the penalty spot.

Whether he thought he deserved a solid round of applause and a quick hug was not clear, but all he got was a heated debate with a City fan (who took exception to the Pole's goading and was then arrested) and then a solid whack from Willie Donachie the next time he took possession of the ball.

Unfortunately for City, the Irish referee noticed both incidents; City were warned about the behaviour of their support and Donachie was shown the red card, allowing him to sit out the embarrassment of a lively, but barren second leg in Łodz where City went out on the away goals rule after a 0–0 draw.

After the Maine Road flop, Tony Book said, 'We have only ourselves to blame. We must not get ourselves involved in situations like we did tonight.' Book's point was a fair one, but it would take City the best part of a quarter of a century to work out how best to heed his wise words.

Stoke City 3, City 1
Division One, 1988

By Boxing Day 1988, City had been back up to the top division and come right back down again. Mel Machin's young guns were firing on all cylinders in an attempt to once again regain top division status. This was also in the middle of the inflatable craze started by City fans. With the Blues lying fourth in the table and very little public transport to aid the exodus of Hollywood stars, monks and vampires heading for Stoke, over 12,000 City supporters in fancy dress turned up to support the team. With the home side giving one end and one side of the ground to City's travelling charabanc, the mass of thousands of yellow bananas was a sight to behold. As the players ran out to a wall of noise, they too held a giant banana each, which were tossed into the partying supporters. At the height of the hooligan problem, Blues supporters were striking back strongly against Margaret Thatcher's anti-football government with a wordless statement that spoke volumes.

Words were also in short supply to describe how, after this tremendous salute from the fans, City could go one up and then be swept away by an average Stoke team containing the likes of John Gidman, Chris Kamara, Peter Beagrie and Tony Henry. But this was classic City territory and the majority of the away supporters leaving at the end – deep sea divers, Rambos and clerics alike – would remember the trip for a long time after the football match had faded from memory. The Blues would end that season with a classic cliff-hanger at Bradford, returning to the Promised Land with less than four minutes to spare thanks to Trevor Morley's last-gasp equaliser.

City 0, Liverpool 5
Division One, 1982
___

Games against Liverpool in the 1970s and '80s usually came with a public health warning for Blues fans, much like home fixtures against Fulham do these days. Although Peter Reid's side struggled gamely to redress the balance, Alan Ball took City right back to those slapstick days in the mid-1990s. Among the many drubbings against Liverpool was a particularly galling 5–0 home defeat in 1982. This was the season after the heroic FA Cup run of 1981, when the newly acquired Trevor Francis would bring the Blues untold fame and fortune. As it panned out, Francis spent most of the season on the treatment table and City fizzled away to a tenth-place finish. By Easter, the slide down the table was in full flow. Liverpool, with the scent of the championship in their nostrils, arrived to deliver the annual Maine Road demolition in frighteningly good form. They had scored sixteen goals against City in the last four fixtures between the sides at Maine Road with a solitary goal in reply. Here they were once again at their inimitable best. That a 40,000 crowd could still see the funny side of things shows that the gulf in class between the sides just wasn't worth worrying about on the day. Liverpool waltzed around Nicky Reid and Kevin Bond at will, scoring through Lee, Neal, Johnston, Kennedy and Rush. As Bob Paisley took off his flat cap at the end and folded it away into his coat pocket, the City fans were still busy running through their repertoire of songs, showing that familiar terrific support during what had been an embarrassing game. Liverpool went on to win the title again and City began preparations for relegation the following season.

City 2, Tottenham Hotspur 4
FA Cup 6th round, March 1993

Two years earlier City had gone into the FA Cup quarter-finals full of the optimism a good cup run brings. Victories over Reading, QPR and Barnsley had led some to think that this was finally the year the Blues went all the way to Wembley, but alas, it was to be another false dawn. With the new Platt Lane Stand opened before the game and a 34,000 sell-out creating a thunderous atmosphere, City were ahead within 10 minutes, as Mike Sheron's thumping header found the target. By the end, however, Spurs had scored four, missed many more than that and there had been a huge pitch invasion from both the Kippax and the sparkling new stand behind the goal. The atmosphere had gone from thunderous to powder keg and City had gone from rampant to flattened. It was somehow typical that Terry Phelan's wonder goal, as he sliced diagonally across the whole length of the pitch to score, should go almost unnoticed in the mayhem of police horses that urinate forever and various other recriminations. A huge manhunt followed the game with mugshots filling the programme and threats of ground closure hanging over the Blues' dismal end to the season. It was clearly another year when City's name was not written on the Cup.

City 0, Arsenal 3
Division One, 1980

By 1980 City's home results were as dire as those away from home and the only pattern one could discern were strings of dreadful and embarrassing defeats. By this time the club was departing the era of Tony Book's strong late 1970s side and were well into Malcolm Allison's money-laden mystery tour. With the likes of Steve Daley, Mike Robinson, Steve Mackenzie and Bobby Shinton already on board at great expense, Big Mal still felt the distinct need to go out and buy in March 1980.

A small space needed to be filled where the hapless Shinton had already departed, shipped out on loan to Millwall, so Allison spent £1.25m on Kevin Reeves from Norwich. The City boss talked up the arrival of the inexperienced Reeves to such an extent that, by the time his debut ended in the ever-so-slight anti-climax of a 3–0 home reverse by Arsenal, Allison had been forced to change tack and was even admitting that he might get the sack.

The irony of his customary press conference cigar and glass of champagne were not lost on onlookers with this truly feeble City performance. Reeves himself added to the fun by missing two presentable chances and giving away the penalty that led to Arsenal's first goal. This was the thirteenth game in a row without a win – the run would last another six games until a comical goal at Wolves, scored by Reeves after Ray Palmer and Paul Bradshaw had performed a music hall routine in front of their own goal allowing the City striker to earn a much-needed victory. For Big Mal the writing was on the wall and within another handful of similarly inept displays he would be on his way out of City the following autumn.

City 2, Chelsea 3
Division One, January 1979

With Maine Road looking like the set from *Ice Station Zebra*, a nervous crowd watched City slither and slide to a truly awful defeat against a Chelsea side slumbering next to bottom in the league. Peter Johnson, in the *Daily Mail*, called Chelsea 'endearingly disorganised', but failed to call up any adjectives which might have suited the home side's sloppiness.

With City bouncing off the twin towers of Micky Droy and Steve Wicks, a comedy on ice was played out before 31,876 feet-stamping punters. City managed to be both 1–0 up and 2–1 up (the second another strike from substitute Ron Futcher) and it was almost inconceivable that the points should go to the London strugglers, but City contrived to do just that and, within three error-strewn minutes, the unthinkable but strangely inevitable had happened.

When Chelsea managed a corner with fifteen minutes to go, the Kippax hooted its derision at a hotch-potch side which had had difficulty exiting its own half for most of the match. Seconds later the home fans watched aghast as Walker's corner was missed by Wicks, outrageously miskicked by the mountainous Droy and finally finished off by Peter Osgood.

Suddenly, a side which had looked timid and hopeless for 75 minutes managed to put Walker away through the middle and, running curiously alone from the half-way line, he slotted home under Corrigan for the most unlikely of wins. With slush and mud everywhere, an orange ball, grey-haired Peter Bonetti repelling everything thrown at him and the most hapless of visitors making off with the points, those left in the ground at the end were not just numb from the weather

Shock! Horror! Elation!
It's the 20 Most Dramatic Season Finales

The Blues have, over the years, had a reputation for making the final game of the campaign a nail-biter – here are twenty occasions when City put their supporters through the mill with incredibly tense last-day dramas.

City v Southampton
11 May 2003
Result Needed: None – last game at Maine Road
Actual Result: 0–1
Drama Factor: ★ Satisfaction: ★ Match rating: ★

The last ever game at Maine Road was bound to be an emotional occasion with dramas all of its own. Nothing hinged on the game, but it was also Shaun Goater's last appearance for the Blues so it was perfectly set-up for a huge anti-climax, which the Blues duly delivered. Ultimately, it was a damp squib of a game that should have been so much more.

Bradford City v City
7 May 1927
Result Needed: Massive win to clinch promotion
Actual Result: 8–0
Drama Factor: ★★ Satisfaction: ★ Match rating: ★★★★

Nobody would have argued City were well worth one of the two promotion spots available. They had played fantastic attacking football and had already 100 goals going into the clash with bottom-of-the-table Bradford City. Portsmouth, on the same points but a better goal average seemed to be in a commanding position, but City ran riot against the Bantams and scored eight without reply ensuring that the race for the final spot would go to the wire. Then news filtered through that, despite City's superior goals scored – 108 to Pompey's 87 – the Fratton Park side's victory meant that their goal average (as opposed to goal difference back then) was 1.7755 and the Blues' was 1.7705 – they had been scuppered by the narrowest margin ever in a promotion race. Ironically, under today's rulings, City would have finished second by virtue of more goals scored.

Manchester United v City
27 April 1974
Result Needed: None – safe in mid-table
Actual Result: 1–0
Drama Factor: ★★ Satisfaction: ★★★★★ Match rating: ★★★★

Perhaps the most famous Manchester derby of the lot, City travelled the short distance to Old Trafford where urban legend will have you believe the Blues sent the Reds down. That's partly true, but United were pretty much condemned anyway, with only a near mathematical miracle and several results going their way possibly saving them. So, technically, yes, we did send them down, though don't they just hate that fact? Denis Law's goal close to full-time settled it.

Oldham Athletic v City
2 May 1992
Result Needed: Win to secure fifth place
Actual Result: 5–2
Drama Factor: ★★ Satisfaction: ★★ Match rating: ★★★★

Goals aplenty at Ice Station Zebra as City secured fifth spot – UEFA Cup football by today's standards – though there was no reward for Peter Reid's side's endeavours on this occasion. The Latics were taken apart by a mixture of raw attacking play and terrific finishing, particularly by David White who scored three of the five goals with Adie Mike and Mike Sheron grabbing the others.

City v Derby County
22 April 1972
Result Needed: None – just pride to play for
Actual Result: 2–0
Drama Factor: ★★ Satisfaction: ★★ Match rating: ★★★

Destiny can take you down various paths and one can only imagine what would have happened to City had they earned just two more points in season 1971/2 and 1976/7. On each occasion, that would have been enough to win the league and the Blues would have secured their place as perhaps the second best side of the entire decade behind Liverpool. This match was academic for City, but not Derby who needed a win to clinch the title. Liverpool and Leeds, a point behind both, had a game to play after the final weekend of the campaign, but neither won and Derby took the title.

City v Sunderland
11 May 1991
Result Needed: A win to finish above United for first time in more than a decade
Actual Result: 3–2
Drama Factor: ★★ Satisfaction: ★★★★ Match rating: ★★★★

As City aimed to finish the campaign on a high, they knew that victory over Sunderland, who were all but relegated, coupled with Manchester United failing to win, and fifth place would be sealed and bragging rights secured for the summer. The Black Cats, backed by 10,000 travelling fans, put up a good fight and came from behind to lead 2–1, but two goals from Niall Quinn gave the points to City and United's loss at Selhurst Park meant a finish above the Reds for the first time since 1978.

Coventry City v City
14 May 1977
Result Needed: None – runners-up spot secured
Actual Result: 1-0
Drama Factor: ★★ Satisfaction: ★ Match rating: ★★★

The Blues couldn't win the title by winning this game and had only their pride to play for after trailing Liverpool by more points than were available. The trip to Coventry proved that City were worthy adversaries to the champions and ended the campaign with only a point separating the top two teams, thanks to Jimmy Conway's solitary goal at Highfield Road.

Stoke City v City
May 1998
Result Needed: Win to avoid relegation
Actual Result: 5–2
Drama Factor: ★★★ Satisfaction: ★ Match rating: ★★★

The vast bank of travelling City fans could take little or no satisfaction from such an emphatic win that ultimately proved futile on a day both the Blues and Stoke were relegated to the nation's third tier. With other teams needing a win all establishing healthy leads by the break, the fate had already been accepted and chants of 'Are you watching Macclesfield?' emanated from the City end as the gallows humour kicked in. Nowhere near as dramatic as it could have been.

Newcastle United v City
1 May 1926
Result Needed: Draw to avoid relegation
Actual Result: 2–3
Drama Factor: ★★★★ Satisfaction: ★ Match rating: ★★★

Newcastle, it seemed, had it in for City. The Geordies had knocked City out of the FA Cup at the semi-final stage just two years earlier and now held the key to the Blues top-flight survival. Having lost the FA Cup Final the previous weekend, City were down but not out and a draw would be enough to remain in the top division and send Burnley down, but it was to be a day of high drama in the north east. City trailed 2–1 when a penalty was awarded – Billy Austin took it, missed and eventually the Blues lost 3–2. Burnley won and the team that had scored just three less than champions, Huddersfield, went down.

City v Newcastle United
7 May 1955
Result Needed: Win to secure FA Cup
Actual Result: 1–3
Drama Factor: ★★★★ Satisfaction: ★ Match rating: ★

Playing in the FA Cup Final is always a fantastic way to end the season – unless you lose, of course, which is what happened on this occasion. Captain Roy Paul had driven his side to the final but it wasn't to be City's day. Jackie Milburn scored after 45 seconds and City lost Jimmy Meadows after 20 minutes and were reduced to ten men. Bobby Johnstone scored on the stroke of half time, but two more goals for the Magpies on 53 and 60 minutes clinched the trophy – their last domestic success, for the Geordies.

City v Middlesbrough
May 2007
Result Needed: Win to secure UEFA Cup spot
Actual Result: 1–1
Drama Factor: ★★★★ Satisfaction: ★ Match rating: ★★★★

Probably the most dramatic last-day match seen at the City of Manchester Stadium thus far, the Blues seemed to be following the script to perfection, despite falling behind to Jimmy Floyd Hasselbaink's thunderous free-kick in the first-half. Kiki Musampa forced an equaliser and with the hosts needing a win to replace Middlesbrough in seventh spot and take the final UEFA Cup spot, David James was used as an emergency striker for the last five minutes. Confusion reigned and the Blues won an injury-time penalty. Robbie Fowler, that denizen of spot-kicks, shot tamely at Mark Schwarzer and a dream ended. What a game. What a crap penalty!

City v Luton Town
14 May 1983
Result Needed: Draw to avoid relegation
Actual Result: 0–1
Drama Factor: ★★★★ Satisfaction: ★ Match rating: ★

No City fan who witnessed this game will ever forget the gut-wrenching feeling after this most dramatic season finale. Needing a point to send Luton Town to Division Two, a struggling City side, backed by a near full-house, seemed to be edging towards a successful conclusion and a chance to rebuild in the summer having maintained their top-flight status. Then, with just four minutes remaining, substitute Raddy Antic drilled a low shot past an unsighted Alex Williams for the cruellest finish imaginable.

City v Liverpool
May 1996
Result Needed: Win to possibly avoid relegation
Actual Result: 2–2
Drama Factor: ★★★★ Satisfaction: ★ Match rating: ★★★

One thing you can usually rely on is that when City need a little help from their friends, they desert us like rats on a sinking ship – a particularly apt description in this instance. Southampton and Coventry were catchable, but if they drew and City drew, City would still go down. The Blues needed a win and the others to draw or lose, but despite fighting back from 2–0 down to level 2–2, it was not enough as both Coventry and the Saints picked up a point. Rumours of late goals against those sides added to the confusion until it was confirmed that Alan Ball's side had lost their battle to stay up on goal difference.

City v Leicester City
29 April 1959
Result Needed: A win to avoid relegation
Actual Result: 3–1
Drama Factor: ★★★★ Satisfaction: ★★★ Match rating: ★★★★

How much satisfaction can actually be gleaned from avoiding relegation is debatable – many would argue it's nothing to celebrate at all. City were fortunate that the fixture list deemed they hold their fate in their own hands with the final two games of the campaign being against the side directly below them and directly above. A point against Joe Mercer's Aston Villa meant a win over Leicester might be enough and in front of almost 47,000 Maine Road fans, goals from McAdams, Hayes and Sambrook were enough to secure a 3–1 win, but with Villa 1–0 up against West Brom, it looked bleak – until the Baggies scored an 88th minute equaliser and condemn Villa to relegation.

Bradford City v City
13 May 1989
Result Needed: A draw to secure promotion
Actual Result: 1–1
Drama Factor: ★★★★ Satisfaction: ★★★★ Match rating: ★★★★

Having blown the chance of winning promotion the previous Saturday against Bournemouth (when a 3–0 lead was blown), City still needed a point to win a place in the top-flight, with Crystal Palace breathing down Mel Machin's side's necks. Of course, City being City, they had to go 1–0 down and wait until the 86th minute to equalise, but that's why we love 'em isn't it? A 1–1 draw was enough and scorer Trevor Morley etched his name into club folklore.

City v Charlton Athletic
11 May 1985
Result Needed: A win to secure promotion
Actual Result: 5–1
Drama Factor: ★★★★ Satisfaction: ★★★★ Match rating: ★★★★★

The sun shining, a packed Maine Road and just two points needed to win promotion – what could possibly go wrong? Well, on this occasion, nothing. It was, as Lou Reed once sang 'a perfect day'. Goals from David Phillips and Andy May made it 2–0 after 15 minutes and three goals in five minutes not long after the break made it 5–0 with just an hour played. It didn't matter that rivals Portsmouth were winning as their goal difference was vastly inferior and the last half-hour became a huge promotion party.

Blackburn Rovers v City
May 2000
Result Needed: A win to secure promotion
Actual Result: 4–1
Drama Factor: ★★★★★ Satisfaction: ★★★★ Match rating: ★★★★★

A truly dramatic match in every sense of the word as City arrived at Ewood Park knowing nothing less than a win would guarantee a second successive promotion. Blackburn, however, weren't prepared to be the patsies and played some of their best football of the season, murdering the Blues in the first half, yet crucially only leading 1–0 at the break. The onslaught continued after the break until Shaun Goater levelled matters to the delight of the 15,000 travelling Blues. An own goal, then strikes from Mark Kennedy and Paul Dickov completed a remarkable turnaround and rendered rivals Ipswich's victory as academic.

City v Gillingham
May 1999
Result Needed: A win to secure promotion
Actual Result: 2–2
Drama Factor: ★★★★★★ Satisfaction: ★★★★ Match rating: ★★★★★

Many would argue that this was the most dramatic final match in the history of the club, but ultimately, the reward was only promotion from Division Two, something that should have been a formality. City very nearly blew it, too, going 2–0 down with just a few minutes left, but the drama of the final six minutes or so will likely never be repeated again, as Kevin Horlock and the Paul Dickov, deep into injury time, made it 2–2. Extra time was something of an anti-climax with penalties almost inevitable, and City doing the business 3–1 completed an amazing, incredible football match – and winning promotion.

City v Birmingham City
5 May 1956
Result Needed: A win to secure the FA Cup
Actual Result: 3–1
Drama Factor: ★★★★ Satisfaction: ★★★★★ Match rating: ★★★★★

The fact that City won the FA Cup for their efforts at Wembley on this occasion edges out the Gillingham match by a whisker.

This game was dramatic for entirely different reasons and with City returning to contest the final for a second successive year, it added extra spice to an already huge day. This time it was City's turn to race into an early lead, courtesy of Joe Hayes' 3rd-minute goal. Birmingham levelled on 15 minutes through Kinsey, but the Blues struck twice in two minutes midway through the second half to establish a 3–1 lead and seemingly an unassailable advantage.

Newcastle United v City
11 May 1968
Result Needed: A win to secure the league title
Actual Result: 4–3
Drama Factor: ★★★★★ Satisfaction: ★★★★★ Match rating: ★★★★★

Quite an incredible season ending, fittingly, with the most dramatic 90 minutes of all and, considering the prize on offer – champions of England – the just winner of the Blues' most breathtaking final matches of the season. The match ebbed and flowed with more twists and turns than an Agatha Christie novel. City knew a win would guarantee them the title, but a draw or loss and a Manchester United win over Sunderland and the title would be heading to Old Trafford, not Maine Road. Mike Summerbee put Joe Mercer's side 1–0 up but Pop Robson equalised within 60 seconds. On the half-hour, Neil Young made it 2–1 but again the hosts equalised within minutes through Jackie Sinclair. Young and Francis Lee scored after the break to make it 4–2, but John McNamee made it 4–3 with five minutes left. City, and their travelling army of around 20,000, endured a nail-biting last few moments before the final whistle went and the title was confirmed. Sunderland's win at United meant nothing – the Blues had won the title on merit rather than default.

Other titles published by The History Press

FEED THE GOAT

SHAUN GOATER WITH DAVID CLAYTON

ISBN 978-0-7509-4871-5

£9.99 Paperback

From humble beginnings in Bermuda, Shaun Goater MBE travelled to England to carve out a successful career in football, becoming a cult hero for Manchester City in the process. His phenomenal goalscoring exploits gave rise to one of the best modern-day terrace chants: 'Feed the Goat and he will score.' Universally respected, a Bermudian legend and a player who refused to give up on his dream, Shaun Goater's story is an inspirational tale for anyone who has faith in their own ability.

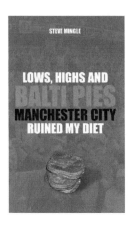

LOWS, HIGHS AND BALTI PIES: MANCHESTER CITY RUINED MY DIET

STEVE MINGLE

ISBN 978-0-7524-3178-9

£9.99 Paperback

What is it about Manchester City? Why can't they ever behave sensibly? How do their famously loyal and long-suffering supporters retain any semblance of sanity? Filled with humour, while infused with an unhealthy, unconditional hatred of a certain other team, Steve Mingle's book provides a highly individual perspective, dating back to 1967.

ALLISON WONDERLAND: MASTERMIND OF MAINE ROAD'S GOLDEN AGE

STEVE MINGLE

ISBN 978-0-7524-4748-1

£9.99 Paperback

Malcom Allison. Inspirational and visionary, charismatic and volatile, arrogant and outspoken. *Allison Wonderland* captures the many facets of one of football's genuine legends, as well as charting the development and decline of his relationship with Joe Mercer. It brings back to life the excitement of City's greatest era: the glorious triumphs, the crushing disappointments and the real story behind where it all went wrong. Some of it might even be true . . .

Visit our website and discover thousands of other History Press books.

www.thehistorypress.co.uk